THE OVERFLOW

Ninety Days of Wisdom, Testimony and Encouragement to Fill You to Overflow

LANELL DRUMMER

The Overflow – Ninety Days of Wisdom, Testimony and Encouragement to Fill You to Overflow

© 2023 Lanell Drummer

Liberty Rain
Liberty2Nations@gmail.com

Published by Kindle Direct Publishing | P.O. Box 81226 | Seattle, Washington 98108

Editing services by Felicia Murrell

Interior design services by Word-2-Kindle | 3419 Virginia Beach Blvd # 301 | Virginia Beach, VA 23452

Print edition ISBN: 9798853847088

Printed in the United States of America

Table of Contents

Day 1- A Love Worthy of Any Price

"Greater love has no one than this, that one lay down his life for his friends" (John 15:13).

Beloved, let us love one another, for love is from God; and everyone who loves is born of God and knows God. The one who does not love does not know God, for God is love (1 John 4:7-8).

That which has your heart will eventually have all of you. That is why it is true that once you fully surrender your heart, following Christ will cost you everything.

Many hear that there is a high price to pay to follow Christ and they fear that they will have to give up all the things they love. What they don't know is that with Jesus the exchange is never forced and always in our favor!

Once we truly know His heart, that thing which we love above all else will be Him and the things which we gave up become nothing more than an afterthought.

Little by little, He will invite us to hand over all that is not according to our make and design and who He has called us to be. This is not to steal from us, but rather so that He can impart to us all that is needed and we can be conformed into His image.

The very core of who God is, is love. He is our Savior, our Healer, our Comforter, and so much more. But those attributes are all a byproduct of His core being of love.

Jesus' death on the cross was the most magnificent, purest act of love known to man, but God is so much greater than that single act. Knowing Him as Savior is just one small part of a God who is bigger than life! Of a God who IS love.

Prayer Focus

Father, may I have a greater awareness of Your infinite love, a love that is worthy of any price.

Day 2- The Eternal Story

And the Word became flesh, and dwelt among us, and we saw His glory, glory as of the only begotten from the Father, full of grace and truth (John 1:14).

Jesus answered and said to him, "Truly, truly, I say to you, unless one is born again he cannot see the kingdom of God" (John 3:3).

The story of the life of Jesus is not just His story, but our story too. By ultimate design, when we walk with Christ, our lives will begin to mirror His as we are conformed into His image.

Jesus humbled Himself and came into our world as a babe, He walked in our shoes and experienced our world the same way we did. He grew and learned and came into the fulfillment of His destiny. And He invites us to take the same journey that He did, but this time into His world, His kingdom.

The access to His world is through new birth, but this time, we are the babe in the manger, and we get to humble ourselves and come to Him naked and vulnerable as a babe. We grow and learn and experience more and more of God's kingdom so that we can one day come into the fulfillment of our destiny.

One day, Jesus, the Bridegroom, will return for His spotless bride. The bride will be spotless because her life will have so resembled that of the Bridegroom that you will no longer be able to tell where the life of the bride ends and that of the Bridegroom begins.

This is the process that is happening even as we speak. This is what it means for Him to live in us and us in Him. This is what it means to be one.

The birth of Jesus was only the entry point for Him, just like our new birth (salvation) is only the entry point for us. That day the manger was the beginning of new life, not just for the Bridegroom, but also for the bride.

What we celebrate as Christmas was and is the ultimate gift, the ultimate love story, and the ultimate invitation to life. It is not only about one day at Christmas, it is about His eternal story and ours.

Prayer Focus

Jesus, thank You for coming and inviting us into Your love story. Thank You for Your great invitation to new life.

Day 3- The Living Will

But now apart from the Law the righteousness of God has been manifested, being witnessed by the Law and the Prophets, even the righteousness of God through faith in Jesus Christ for all those who believe; for there is no distinction; for all have sinned and fall short of the glory of God, being justified as a gift by His grace through the redemption which is in Christ Jesus (Romans 3:21-24).

While a man is living, he plans for the future of his family.

He will often draw up a will, a binding contract of what is to happen upon his death. The contract will note what rightfully belongs to which family members and when and how they are to come into this inheritance.

But what happens when there is no knowledge of that will? If it gets lost or stolen or a fake will is substituted in its place? Then the rights that were lawfully meant for the family members are lost. The loved ones will live never knowing the good things that were left for them, what their legal rights were, or the heart of the giver.

Jesus drew up a will that explained what was to happen upon His death. The world's sins went to trial, a sentence was passed, and justice was served through the contract signed upon Jesus' death on the cross.

With all of that said, one might wonder why sin still wreaks havoc on our society? It does so because few have knowledge of or demand the upholding of the legal rights that were paid for at the cross. How do we know this? Because much of the church is still crying out for a trial and for justice to be paid.

The enemy has sown the biggest lie that says there is no will, so you yourselves must pay the price and the people and nations must still stand trial.

As the church, we were left as executors of Jesus' will. It is our job to know what has legally transpired through Christ's death, to make known the presence of His will, to wave the will in the enemy's face and say, here is the legal binding contract that Christ established before His death and these are our rights.

As executors of the will of Christ, it is the job of the sons and daughters of Christ to stand against the enemy and make the decree that brings heaven's justice here to Earth. To declare the truth to the enemy and to the storms. To see that the justice that was already established is played out on the Earth.

My friends, we must know the goodness of this will called grace. We must know what legal rights were bought for us, and we must learn to be executors of that will.

It is only through our execution of the will of Christ that justice on earth will begin to look like justice in heaven. We must educate ourselves so that we can take hold of the beautiful justice of Christ. Our inheritance depends on it!

Prayer Focus

God, help me to fully grasp the goodness of your grace, to understand the fullness of your covenant and what was given to me through the person of Jesus Christ.

Day 4- The Good Shepherd

The LORD is my shepherd, I shall not want. He makes me lie down in green pastures; He leads me beside quiet waters. He restores my soul; He guides me in the paths of righteousness For His name's sake (Psalms 23:1-3).

When I lived in Northern California, I used to go to a prayer room on Thursday mornings. It was about forty minutes away, so I normally stayed a few hours. But one morning, after about an hour, I felt a gentle prompt to leave.

At the time, I was working to be better about listening to those small nudges, even when I didn't understand. So I got up and quietly made my way out.

Since I now had extra time, I decided to go by this store in the mall and pick up something I needed. I drove over to the mall, but it wasn't open yet.

As I pulled out of the parking lot, the Holy Spirit said to go to the bank. Admittedly, I only had a few dollars in my wallet, but it wasn't something I would have stopped for. But again, I was trying to be quick about following God's still small voice.

I got the money and circled around the parking lot. There, sitting on the corner in the grass was a man with his head down. He had a sign at his feet saying he needed bus fare. I didn't know how long he had been there, possibly since the night before, but he had obviously given up on anyone stopping.

I pulled over and called him over to the car, only to be surprised. This was no man; this was a boy about fifteen or sixteen years old. Someone's baby out there by himself on the corner.

I tried to communicate with him only to discover he was mute. But when I handed him the money I had just moments before pulled out the bank, the look of disbelief and gratefulness and the tears that sprang to his eyes said it all.

I imagine a thousand cars probably passed him by that morning as people rushed off to work. And it made me smile to think God called me out of worship in the prayer room and sent me on a seemingly fruitless errand, all to land me in front of this boy who needed a way back home.

But that is how the Father loves, and He is always looking to get us back home.

Sometimes ministry is not about the programs and services. Sometimes it is just about listening to His still small voice and stopping for the one He has placed in front of us.

Prayer Focus

God, help me to follow your lead even when I do not understand. Thank You that You are our Good Shepherd and are faithful to lead us as we should go.

Day 5- Seeking Christ

"Many will say to Me on that day, 'Lord, Lord, did we not prophesy in Your name, and in Your name cast out demons, and in Your name perform many miracles?' And then I will declare to them, 'I never knew you; DEPART FROM ME, YOU WHO PRACTICE LAWLESSNESS'" (Mathew 7:22-23).

"If anyone hears My sayings and does not keep them, I do not judge him; for I did not come to judge the world, but to save the world" (John 12:47).

"And whoever in the name of a disciple gives to one of these little ones even a cup of cold water to drink, truly I say to you, he shall not lose his reward" (Mathew 10:42).

Rarely is Christ found in the popular opinion. Because things like praying for and loving your enemies, giving to the poor, welcoming the foreigner, loving your neighbor as yourself, and sacrificing your rights, freedom and comfort for others are not popular things.

Beware of a gospel that justifies the setting aside of the true tenants of Christianity, even one that can produce miracles, signs and wonders.

Miracles are not a sign of true relationship with Christ.

A gospel built around miracles will always have an abundance of fair-weather converts along for the ride as long as it is benefiting them. But they will be incapable of giving a drink of cool water to the dying world.

Jesus came to save the world. It's easy to say we are a follower of Christ, but the true test of that will be in how we treat and love the world He gave everything to save.

Prayer Focus

Jesus, give me a heart for the world you came to save. Let me seek to be a follower of You, not just a seeker of miracles.

Day 6- God's Masterpiece

For we are His workmanship, created in Christ Jesus for good works, which God prepared beforehand so that we would walk in them (Ephesians 2:10).

For I am confident of this very thing, that He who began a good work in you will perfect it until the day of Christ Jesus (Philippians 1:6).

During corporate prayer one day, someone came forward and prayed that God would rend the heavens.

And as soon as they said the word rend, I heard a play on the word, and God said to me that now is the time that He would render.

For those unfamiliar with the term render, it is a term of creation often used in things like video production. The creator will take a bunch of individually edited pieces, video clips, special effects, photos, audio, etc. and pull them all together to make a final video.

Often in life, we walk through times where it can seem like our life is disconnected and meaningless because we have only been able to see our life as an individual piece. Yet, your life has been created to function in line with other pieces in order to be a complete masterpiece.

A three second special effect apart from the whole video is meaningless. However, when properly placed, synced and allowed to play with the other components, it can make or break a video.

Today, you may feel like you are stuck in edit mode. Constantly being clipped, stretched and adjusted. But God is not finished yet. He has a promise over your life to render and release a final product! Hold onto that promise for His masterpiece will not disappoint!

Prayer Focus

God, help me to stand in your faithfulness, and rest in the knowledge that You will complete the work that You have started in me, fashioning me into Your masterpiece.

Day 7- Lost Broken and Lonely to Loved

"Let the beloved of the LORD rest secure in him, for he shields him all day long, and the one the LORD loves rests between his shoulders" (Deuteronomy 33:12 NIV).

In 2013, I had a dream where a group of us were out on the street walking home when this big dog approached.

He was filthy, unattractive, and his body was greatly distorted. He looked like he had been run over by a truck and crushed.

Upon seeing the dog, almost everyone in the group took a step back, scared he was going to attack. But from this group, one woman emerged. She held out her hand, and at first it looked like the dog considered attacking, but then instead, he licked her hand.

She then reached down and picked him up, cradling him like he was her most beloved baby.

In the dream, I wept and wept at how she loved the dog, and then I woke up feeling the overwhelming love of the Father wash over me.

This dream was both a picture of how the Father sees and adores us, and also of how we should see and adore one another.

The more hurt, broken and lost we are, the more unattractive we may appear to man, and the more man will fear us. But the kind of love that sees past the outward appearance, that will cradle the beloved, even in their most distorted form, is the kind of love that will change the narrative from lost to found, from broken to healed, and from lonely to loved. This is the love of the Father.

Prayer Focus

God, help me to look upon my fellow man and myself with eyes like yours, eyes that see each one as worthy, precious, and beloved.

Day 8- New Lenses

Husbands, love your wives, just as Christ also loved the church and gave Himself up for her, so that He might sanctify her, having cleansed her by the washing of water with the word, that He might present to Himself the church in all her glory, having no spot or wrinkle or any such thing; but that she would be holy and blameless (Ephesians 5:25-27).

One night, I dreamt there were many family members over to my house. After everyone had gone home, I saw that they had left behind many pairs of sunglasses all over the floor.

The glasses were all different shapes and colors. I remember thinking maybe I would put them away and people would come back for them, but I knew in my heart that they would not return for them.

I opened a drawer where I put these glasses, along with others, and I looked them over. Some were missing lenses, some oddly shaped, or outdated and broken. The glasses in the drawer were no longer useful or attractive, and none of them were as good as the updated pair that I had.

From this, God began to speak to me saying the old, broken and outdated perspectives of who Christ is, and who His church is, will be left behind.

Christ is re-aligning his church. As that happens, the old ways will become less attractive and many will leave them behind for a better more useful and attractive perspective.

This is not a weakening of the church, but a strengthening!

Prayer Focus

Jesus, help us to trust You to strengthen and bring needed change to Your church. Let us not fear the changes, but rather to open our heart as You build Your glorious church.

Day 9- Lights in Darkness

"You are the light of the world. A city set on a hill cannot be hidden; nor does anyone light a lamp and put it under a basket, but on the lampstand, and it gives light to all who are in the house. Let your light shine before men in such a way that they may see your good works, and glorify your Father who is in heaven" (Mathew 5:14-16).

And He said to them, "Go into all the world and preach the gospel to all creation" (Mark 16:15).

A common misperception in today's church has been that we are to build this sterile life where we separate ourselves from all darkness.

But the goal has never been for us to run from or separate ourselves from darkness. Quite the opposite. The goal has been for us to go into the dark places and transform the darkness to light.

So many in the church live lives where they are struggling to find fulfillment and purpose because they are trying to shine in a church building full of other lights.

Adding another light to a room that is already lit, makes little difference. The 500th lamp to a lamp store yields no noticeable difference from when the store only had 499 lamps.

This reality can lead to people feeling powerless or being unaware of the power and impact they truly carry. Because it is only when you add light to a place of darkness that its true power and effectiveness can be seen.

The church will not learn who they truly are in Christ until they go out into the field of darkness and do what they were created to do—shine.

The gathering place of the saints was never meant to be substituted for a mission field. In a lot of ways, we do a disservice when we have a singular focus within, building walls and encouraging people to remove and separate their gifts from the world and bring them to be used solely at the church house. This results in church buildings full of dissatisfied, unfulfilled people all competing to get to shine and the turning of the church into one of the most competitive places around.

There are those called to serve within church buildings, but we should also be sending people out and encouraging them to use their gifts in the world where they can fulfill their purpose of being a light in darkness.

Go out and shine bright, my friends!

Prayer Focus

Jesus, stir my heart to go forth boldly into the world and share the gospel. Let me not keep my light to myself.

Day 10- The Overflow

You prepare a table before me in the presence of my enemies; You have anointed my head with oil; My cup overflows (Psalm 23:5).

"And the LORD will continually guide you, And satisfy your desire in scorched places, And give strength to your bones; And you will be like a watered garden, And like a spring of water whose waters do not fail" (Isaiah 58:11).

"He who believes in Me, as the Scripture said, 'From his innermost being will flow rivers of living water'" (John 7:38).

Years ago, God showed me an illustration. I was filling up a bottle and noticed there were some soap suds left in the bottle.

My first attempt was to tip the bottle and pour the suds outs, but when I tipped the bottle, the suds just went to the back of the bottle and the water I wanted to keep poured out instead. In fact, some of the soap suds remained in the bottom even after all the water was poured out.

In that moment, God reminded me that there was an easier and less wasteful way to accomplish what I wanted. If I let the water fill to overflow, the suds would rise to the top and would empty out first, rather than last.

He then showed me that this is the place most of his people live from. We want so badly to get what is in us out to the world, dreaming of revival in our hearts, and in others. But we keep tipping our cups.

God is faithful to pour into us, but we have not learned to properly rest in Him to the point where we fill to overflow. Tipping the cup completely empties us out of even what we need to hold onto, and sometimes even still, we never manage to get out of us all we hoped to release.

This practice causes us to start over from the beginning time and time again, and makes us vulnerable and frustrated in the process.

Rest is so vital to fulfilling God's plans for us.

We often forget that things operate differently in the kingdom of God. We sing songs asking God to empty us so that we can be filled. But that is man's way, not God's.

God has no need to take us to empty to refill us any more than a good potter needs to discard the clay, or a goldsmith needs to pour out the impure gold. Rather, a potter will reshape the clay, and a goldsmith will skim the impurities off the top, preserving the purer gold beneath.

God's way is for us to trust and rest more in Him so that when it is time to do what He asks, it takes less work, time and effort and we are not left with feeling empty, burnt out and frustrated.

When we rest in Him, all the stresses, impurities, and things that are not of Him rise to the top where He so gently washes them away.

Prayer Focus

God, help me to be patient, and learn to rest in You and let You fill me to overflow.

Day 11- Royalty Everyday

"The LORD your God is with you, the Mighty Warrior who saves. He will take great delight in you; in his love he will no longer rebuke you, but will rejoice over you with singing." (Zephaniah 3:17, NIV).

You will also be a crown of beauty in the hand of the LORD, And a royal diadem in the hand of your God (Isaiah 62:3).

Our church congregation was once challenged to take twenty-eight days and stand before the mirror and ask God what He thinks about us.

When the challenge was extended, I immediately thought well He is going to say the same thing about me that He does about everyone. After all, He is crazy in love with each and every one of us. So, I really had no intention on asking God the question.

But the following morning, the Father awakened me and decided He was going to answer the question I wouldn't ask. He said, remember how you felt on your birthday this year? It wasn't really a question. He knew very well that I remembered.

You see, growing up, my family was never big on birthday celebrations. I can only remember having one adult birthday party thrown many years prior by a few friends from church, not by my family.

But that year was different. I celebrated my birthday in a foreign country with new friends that I had only known for three weeks, so I had not anticipated a celebration of any kind that year, let alone what I received.

The day started with birthday songs and dances, and dozens of birthday hugs and blessings from my new community of people. There were homemade birthday cards with personal notes written in them, even a birthday cake!

Did I remember how I felt? Of course I did! In the beginning it was this strange and foreign mix of awe, delight, and embarrassment that people were making a fuss celebrating me. But by the end of the day, I just felt like royalty.

And that night for dinner, without anyone knowing it, they served my favorite dish. I knew it was a birthday kiss from my Father in heaven.

That day after answering my unasked question, the Father said to me, this is how I celebrate you every day. And my heart felt a little bit bigger that morning.

God's love for us is personal, full of personal love notes and favorite things. He takes note of what we delight in. While He loves each one of us passionately, we each stand alone in His sight as He carries out our cake in celebration of who we are. Each one of us are royalty each and every day, the question is whether or not we know it. Today, and every day, He celebrates you!

Prayer Focus

Father, let Your love and delight in me become an undeniable truth in my heart.

Day 12- Promises and Giants

'For I know the plans that I have for you,' declares the LORD, 'plans for welfare and not for calamity to give you a future and a hope' (Jeremiah 29:11).

"No weapon that is formed against you will prosper; And every tongue that accuses you in judgment you will condemn. This is the heritage of the servants of the LORD, And their vindication is from Me," declares the LORD (Isaiah 54:17).

Then Caleb quieted the people before Moses and said, "We should by all means go up and take possession of it, for we will surely overcome it" (Numbers 13:30).

Our mindsets and beliefs, the words from our lips, and the action of our hands all mold and shape our outcome.

In the Bible, the book of Numbers tells the story of twelve leaders of the tribes of Israel sent to spy out the promised land of Canaan. Ten of the spies came back reporting what they saw as sure defeat if they went into the land. Only two of the leaders believed they could overcome and said there is fruit to be had, let us go and possess the land.

In our world today, we often live a twelve spy situation with the majority focused on the giants and the potential calamity. Many become hyper-focused on issues until those issues look larger than everything else. They see themselves as smaller than the opposing factors, powerless, and ripe to be trampled on.

But God has called for His remnant to step forward. The two, out of twelve spies, who can look out on the land and not focus on the giants, but rather on the fruit to be had and the promises God has given.

The twelve spies all viewed the same situation, a very real situation, but only two could see that grim looking or not, outnumbered or not, there was still victory available!

Victory is often only be achieved by those who not only can see past the giants, but are willing to risk and go after the fruit.

You must know in your heart that God is bigger than any giant!

As God's people, we must learn to fix our eyes on His promises. Those promises have not changed. Will we believe, act and move upon them, even in the face of what looks contrary?

There is much fruit to be had, let us go forward into the land!

Prayer Focus

God, help me to see with eyes of victory! Let there be no doubt in my heart that You are bigger than any obstacle that stands between me and my destiny.

Day 13- Making the Impossible Possible

The LORD said, "Behold, they are one people, and they all have the same language. And this is what they began to do, and now nothing which they purpose to do will be impossible for them" (Genesis 11:6).

For just as we have many members in one body and all the members do not have the same function, so we, who are many, are one body in Christ, and individually members one of another (Romans 12:4-5).

And looking at them Jesus said to them, "With people this is impossible, but with God all things are possible" (Mathew 19:26).

God revealed one of the greatest secrets to success in the first book of Genesis.

The people of the land were unified and all spoke the same language, and God himself said that because of this, nothing they set out to do would be impossible. Nothing!

Where there is unity, one person's weaknesses are covered by another's strengths, and this brings infinite possibilities.

And where there is unity, there is no competition, and an environment void of competition empowers all members and encourages growth.

It was a breakdown of the ability to communicate and the loss of unity that separated the people into nations, and only restoration of unity of purpose and communication brings the nations together.

The key to making the impossible possible has always been to unify, to have a common agenda, to dispose of the mindset of division and be united under a common objective. To be one body.

Although they moved apart from God, and their motive may not have been entirely pure, the people of that day knew they could reach the heavens and that there were no limits to what they could do in their unified state.

The potential to reach the heavens remains today for those willing to lay down their personal agendas and unify in Christ! You will not reach the heavens without Him, but with Him, all things are possible!

Prayer Focus

God, help me to walk with others in unity, to lay down any areas in my heart that hold division.

Day 14- The Choice

He was oppressed and He was afflicted, Yet He did not open His mouth; Like a lamb that is led to slaughter, And like a sheep that is silent before its shearers, So He did not open His mouth (Isaiah 53:7).

But Jesus was saying, "Father, forgive them; for they do not know what they are doing" (Luke 23:34).

Right out of college I went to work at a hospital as a Patient Care Technician. The hospital I worked at served quite a large geographical area, and was the closest hospital to a lot of the more isolated mountain communities.

One day, accompanied by her two grown sons and a husband, this woman was admitted. They had traveled quite a distance from the mountains to come to the hospital.

I was working a 7 a.m. to 7 p.m. shift that day so my first encounter with her was at breakfast time.

The cafeteria had just delivered her meal tray, but she did not eat her breakfast that day. Instead, she and one of her sons threw her breakfast at me as they hurled curses, threats and racial slurs.

I managed to dodge the hot coffee and most of the food and make it out the room mostly unscathed.

The nursing supervisor and I discussed the incident, and she asked me what I wanted to do. The choices ranged anywhere from filing a police report against them, switching the woman's care to someone else, or enduring the battle.

We all have choices in life and defining moments where we decide who we are going to be.

That day, I decided not to take the bait, but instead to endure. Offense is a choice. They called me dirty, an animal, a whore and many other things that I knew I was not, and lunch played out much the same as breakfast.

But by the third meal, that woman got hungry, hungry enough to eat her meal instead of throwing it at me. And by day three, she wanted a bath enough to allow me into her presence to assist.

Before her discharge at the end of the week, her family asked to speak with me. I was a bit wary, but I returned to the room to meet with the entire family. And to my surprise, they all took turns apologizing for their actions. Actions that were based out of fear of the unknown.

You see, I was the first African-American person they had encountered in person in their lives and maybe the only one they ever would.

Afterwards, I couldn't help but realize the opportunity I had been given. An opportunity to shape their view of my race for the rest of their lives. I thought about how it would have turned out differently had I chosen to press charges with the police, cursed back, or walked away that first day.

We have a lot of similar choices when it comes to our faith. For some, we may be the only representation of Christ many will ever encounter. And how we choose to relate and react to others shapes people's view of all who call themselves followers of Christ.

If God is ever going to be able to use us to bring freedom and life to the world, we cannot allow offense to be a part of the equation. God wants to be able to trust us to go into the uncharted places. Places where there may be fear of the unknown that brings threats and negative reaction.

Until we set our hearts to choose love in all situations, we cannot fully be used of God. The choice is ours and ours alone.

Prayer Focus

God, help me to make the choice to not walk in offense, to love even in the face of opposition and persecution.

Day 15- The Great Mirror

A man's discretion makes him slow to anger, And it is his glory to overlook a transgression (Proverbs 19:11).

A brother offended is harder to be won than a strong city, And contentions are like the bars of a citadel (Proverbs 18:19).

Life presents us with offensive things. But offense is nothing more than a mirror held to our own heart.

Jesus never worried about offense because offense is not a God-given emotion. It is a symptom of deeper heart issues and a weakness in identity.

There is a passage in the book of Matthew where a Canaanite woman cries out to Jesus asking him to heal her daughter. And no matter how many times I read the account, I am always fascinated by this exchange where Jesus responds and tells the woman, *"It is not good to take the children's bread and throw it to the dogs" (Mathew 15:26).*

It fascinates me because this woman had every right to be offended by his words. But he chose those words specifically to reveal her heart, knowing the world's view of her was as someone lesser than and no better than a dog.

But the amazing thing is that she chose to ignore the door to offense and instead used his statement to her benefit as a springboard to a greater position. In verse 27, she gives the iconic response of *"Yes, Lord; but even the dogs feed on the crumbs which fall from their masters' table."*

Her choice to not be distracted by offense allowed her the great opportunity to grab hold of benefits that otherwise wouldn't have been available to her at that time. Benefits only her real identity could procure.

People may not see your worth. They may call you degrading names. But when the door to offense is presented, it is always an opportunity to take a higher position and receive greater things in return.

Jesus was called a drunk, a blasphemer, belittled as nothing more than the carpenter's son, and a Nazarene at that. But he never took offense. He didn't stage a protest on people's low view of carpenters or Nazarenes or even respond to the allegations at all, because he knew fully well his own identity and his own worth.

We must remember that if we have our identity in Christ, the blood of Christ speaks a better word over us than any word of our enemies. You only have to choose to apply Christ's blood, his identity, and who he says you are instead of taking on that which keeps you bound in an old identity.

The door to offense can be your distraction, or it can be your springboard to go higher into your identity in Christ.

Prayer Focus

God, help me to view offensive things differently. Help me to use them as a mirror showing me where I am not standing firmly in my identity in Christ.

Day 16- Free from Bondage

It was for freedom that Christ set us free; therefore keep standing firm and do not be subject again to a yoke of slavery (Galatians 5:1).

There is a cost to obtaining and maintaining freedom.

For those of us in Christ, that cost often lies in letting go of our self-efforts, and in keeping ourselves free so that we can enjoy the freedoms Christ has already paid for.

We have to learn to let go of the things that unnecessarily bind like setting unnecessary rules, expectations and pressures that hinder, so we can move with the Holy Spirit. And we have to learn to say no to that which doesn't belong to us so that we can say yes to that which does!

Many things look good on the surface but have control and manipulation weaved through its core, whether intentional or not. And this can place us in boxes we were never meant to be put in.

No matter how "godly" or attractive an opportunity looks, it is never God's intent that we return to the enslavement that past places of bondage had to offer. Those places often present themselves as a quick fix to our most immediate problems or perceived lack. We look to past bondage for its quick solution, while ignoring all the red flags of how it will strip us of our freedom.

We should always count the costs. Anything that requires us to trade one freedom for others will build a wall around our heart that is much harder to recover from than staying free in the first place!

We can rest assured that the Father withholds no good thing from His children. If God is specifically saying no to something, it may very well be bondage in disguise.

Prayer Focus

God, help me to have no doubt that Your heart is for me. Let me rest assured that if You are saying no, that it is for my good. Help me to not pick back up those things that held me captive and to live in the full freedom of Christ.

Day 17- Like a New Babe

Yet You are He who brought me forth from the womb; You made me trust when upon my mother's breasts. Upon You I was cast from birth; You have been my God from my mother's womb (Psalm 22:9-10).

I was in a half-awake state one morning when I had the flash of a picture before my eyes. It was of a mother breastfeeding her child. Something so simple and beautiful. In the moment, the Lord spoke to my heart saying, this is the level of intimacy that I want with my children.

There is a special bond of intimacy formed between a mother and a child at her breast, or even a child on their father's chest. It is a bond that by design was meant for every child, male or female, rich or poor.

To lay in your creator's arms and receive from their own body and be cradled in their love is intimacy at its greatest.

A mother's milk sustains life and provides all the nutrients a child needs. There are replacements, but none quite as good. Strength and immunity are passed from the mother to her child at each intimate feeding. And beyond this, even skin to skin contact with mother or father has been found to strengthen a baby's digestive and immune systems.

This transfer by intimate contact doesn't just happen in the natural. It also happens in the spiritual between man and God, our Creator.

Our Father invites us to let Him provide the nourishment, protection and love we need. It is found in its greatest form one on one, in His arms. There is no substitute that can compare.

One of God's names is El Shaddai, which in Hebrew can be translated—the Many Breasted One. He offers a place of intimacy, nourishment, strength and protection for each one who will draw near to partake of Him.

Prayer Focus

Father, draw near to me and help me draw near to you that I might know Your intimacy and hear Your heartbeat which will sustain life.

Day 18- God My Provider

Delight yourself in the LORD; And He will give you the desires of your heart (Psalm 37:4).

"Consider the ravens, for they neither sow nor reap; they have no storeroom nor barn, and yet God feeds them; how much more valuable you are than the birds! (Luke 12:24).

One night I was on a road trip back from the Bay Area. I hadn't eaten since morning and really needed to stop but did not want greasy fast-food. I told the Father what I wanted to eat and began to keep an eye on the restaurant signs, believing God would provide it.

A few hours went by, and I still had not come upon the restaurant. It was approaching 9 p.m. so I decided I was just going to have to choose something else. I pulled into a fast-food restaurant and bought food I didn't want and went back to the car to eat.

I threw up a quick and pretty ungrateful prayer, and then took the first bite. It was so dissatisfying.

At that moment, I looked up, and there on the side of the building next door was a sign for the restaurant I was hoping for.

God spoke then, very gently, and asked, "Why do you still doubt me?"

It was a question that consumed me the rest of the night and even into the next morning. The question wasn't really about my dinner. It was about my greater struggle with doubt as I walked through the process of breaking free of my dependence on myself and on the world's provision and trusting Him completely.

It was also a reminder that our Father is not just concerned about our basic needs. He is also concerned about the desires of our heart.

Sometimes when the expected hour has passed, we give up and turn back to our own devices. But God wants us to hang on and press through even when it looks like He has failed to come through, for we will never be satisfied with the results when we get impatient and jump in to work things out for ourselves.

Impatience and doubt will always cost us something. That day on the road it cost me wasted money and dissatisfaction, and a humbling when I saw, a moment too late, that God had indeed put before me what I had been hoping for.

Prayer Focus

God, thank You that you are a good Father. Help me to rest and trust that no matter what the circumstances may look like, You will be there to care for me.

Day 19- Lay Down Your Burden

Cast your burden upon the LORD and He will sustain you; He will never allow the righteous to be shaken (Psalm 55:22).

Blessed be the Lord, who daily bears our burden, The God who is our salvation. Selah (Psalm 68:19).

'Do not fear, for I am with you; Do not anxiously look about you, for I am your God. I will strengthen you, surely I will help you, Surely I will uphold you with My righteous right hand' (Isaiah 41:10).

God's mercy and desire to see us whole is unrelenting. The picture of salvation is a picture of wholeness.

One night a woman came to the healing rooms where I volunteered. When she walked in the room, I was taken aback by the physical pain I could feel. It took a couple minutes of praying just for me to be able to concentrate past the deep emotional pain in the room and the physical effects it was having on my own body. She was so hurt that she couldn't even speak. She could only cry, and it was heartbreaking to see the hopelessness in her eyes.

The Holy Spirit began to reveal one by one the things to pray for to bring hope and life.

At first, it all seemed to fall on deaf ears because she was so cloaked in her pain. But eventually, God's truth began to break through and she began to nod her head as she listened. By the end of the session, we even got a few smiles and a laugh out that woman. But the most beautiful part was to look in her eyes and see hope looking back.

As shocking as it sometimes can be, I actually like that God sometimes allows me to feel the pain of the people I pray for, because it dispels the lie that God doesn't feel our pain or that He could ever turn a blind eye to it.

He very much wants us to be free from our hurts and pain. Don't be afraid to give your burdens to Him, even if you don't have the words to speak, He knows exactly what you need and is relentless in His efforts to supply it.

Prayer Focus

God, thank You that You see our hurts and struggles, and that You are not immune to our pain. Teach me to let go of my burdens and trust you to bring me to healing and wholeness.

Day 20- A Love that Never Fails

Love never fails (1 Corinthians 13:8).

And we know that God causes all things to work together for good to those who love God, to those who are called according to His purpose (Romans 8:28).

Can we put conditions on our love and still claim to be loving with the love of Christ?

Is our love today only for those who will return it, for the safe, or for the one who won't betray?

Love has always required risk. The risk is that sometimes you will love and your Judas will remain a Judas even after loving him as your own, allowing him into your heart and your space, and letting him drink from your cup.

But sometimes your Judas will turn out to be an Apostle Paul, and their encounter with Christ will lead to a shift in allegiance and life-altering change.

How can we know the difference? We can't. That is the risk that love demands. The same risk that Christ took with each one of us, that we might not love Him back. Yet with Judas, and with each one of us, He is left blameless because He pours out His love unconditionally.

Judas could make no claim that Jesus treated him different than the others, or that He withheld from him because of his past or because of lack of trust.

I believe that Jesus gave His all to Judas up until the end to leave every opportunity for Judas to turn from his path of destruction and choose life. I believe He hoped until the very last second that Judas would have a change of heart. What love! To Jesus, Judas was worth the risk.

What is love, except that one would be willing to lay down his life for another? Jesus had full faith in the outcome and full faith in the power of love. He trusted that no matter the circumstances, that God was good, that God would use the circumstances for his purposes, and that the overall outcome would be for the good of everyone. That assurance is given to each and every one of us.

The reality is, sometimes loving God and loving others will cause you to make decisions that put yourself and your family at higher risk. But can we still give our all to the dark of heart? That is what true love, the love of Christ is about. Whether a Paul or a Judas, a murderer or a priest, a Christian or an unbeliever, each life is worth laying down your own for, that is the love of Christ.

In the end, Judas still chose to betray Christ. But there is no way he went away unaffected by that love. Jesus' sacrificial act of loving Judas was not in vain. It was that very act of betrayal that God used to make a way for all of us to receive a new covenant of love.

The promise is that love never fails. For love to fail, God would have to fail, because He Himself is that love. It is God Himself you are pouring out as that thing we call love. We can love even the riskiest, holding onto the promise that it won't fail. It may not turn out the way we hope or envision, our Judas may betray us after all, but love Himself will never fail us!

Prayer Focus

God, help me to love with an unconditional love, and to trust that Your love never fails, and is worth it even when others don't choose to love back.

Day 21- Weapons of Power

For the weapons of our warfare are not of the flesh, but divinely powerful for the destruction of fortresses (2 Corinthians 10:4).

One night, I took a very delayed flight home from the east coast back to Los Angeles. After deplaning, I arrived to the shuttle bus stop to find the mad chaos of an LAX war zone.

It was a late-night mix of cursing, screaming, stress smoking, and even some tears as people found themselves stranded at the airport because there were more reservations than they could accommodate and few alternative options at that late hour.

In the face of the chaos, I had a choice to make in how I would respond.

I stepped forward and found myself face to face with the ring leader of the chaos. She was armed with a cigarette and every foul word she could think of to yell. We stepped to the side and she told me of her horrendous two-day travel ordeal of cancelled flights and airline ugliness, and I knew she just needed someone to hear her and tell her they understood. Unfortunately, that person was not the lone twenty-year-old girl left to man the angry mob at the shuttle stop.

While her weapons were curse words, I had very different weapons at my disposal. Weapons of peace and joy, and within a few minutes, I had her laughing and jokingly dancing around.

When my ride came, I decided to sacrifice it to this woman and her husband to get home. I then moved to the poor twenty-year-old still hiding after her encounter with the woman I had just put in my ride. She told me that she had been getting cursed out all day long, and that she hated her job.

She asked me why I was not yelling at her like the others, and said, If I were you, I would be mad. But I wasn't there to dish out more strife. Instead, I found myself going from person to person trying to help. I couldn't provide the ride they needed, but I could let them know they were seen and heard and reassure them that all would be ok. It wasn't long before the atmosphere had completely shifted from what it had been when I arrived.

I ended up being the last one to get a ride home, at what was then 5:30 a.m. to my body. I wanted to complain, but then God spoke to my heart some very wise words that I have never forgotten.

He said, you never know who you are until you are in the center of a battle. It is only in the battle that a man finds out the usefulness of the weapons he carries and whether or not he has what it takes to wield those weapons.

He said, the battle never comes at an opportune time and a sacrifice is only a sacrifice if you are giving away what is of value and is rightfully yours. The greatest gain is made by the choices made in the weary times, not when all is well. Lastly, he said, faith and character are only truly seen when we are pressed down and squeezed.

Life will present us with plenty of battles. In those times, we must remember the powerful weapons we have on hand!

Prayer Focus

God, when life presents battles, help me to choose wisely and remember the powerful weapons I have on hand.

Day 22- Good Samaritans

"But a Samaritan, who was on a journey, came upon him; and when he saw him, he felt compassion, and came to him and bandaged up his wounds, pouring oil and wine on them; and he put him on his own beast, and brought him to an inn and took care of him (Luke 10:33-34).

Therefore if anyone is in Christ, he is a new creature; the old things passed away; behold, new things have come (2 Corinthians 5:17).

For all of you who were baptized into Christ have clothed yourselves with Christ. There is neither Jew nor Greek, there is neither slave nor free man, there is neither male nor female; for you are all one in Christ Jesus (Galatians 3:27-28).

In 2015, God woke me up one morning with the word that it is the Samaritan who will bring healing to the nations.

What he meant by the Samaritan is the person whose heart is no longer Jew or Christian, Western or Eastern, White or Black, American, European or Middle-Eastern. The person whose loyalty lies with humanity as a whole and no longer has the lines of division in their heart.

Samaritans are considered neither Jew nor Gentile, but a mixed race. In the bible parable, it was the Good Samaritan (a picture of Jesus) who poured wine and oil in the man's wounds and bandaged them.

The good Samaritans of our day are those who live as new creations, no longer holding to their own race or nationality, but as a new mixed singular race. And this lack of division in their hearts will enable them to pour out the wine and oil and bring healing to the nations.

Even within today's church, most are still trying to decide where their loyalties lie, where they identify, and whose job it is to respond to the situations of our day. Many are just quickly trying to cross to the other side of the street so that they don't have to get involved.

But God is calling out for the Samaritans to arise! The world needs you! You were created and called for such a time as this!

Prayer Focus

Jesus, help me to live as a new creation, one who will love and give my life for the world as you gave your life for the world.

Day 23- Compassion, Mercy and Grace

For we do not have a high priest who cannot sympathize with our weaknesses, but One who has been tempted in all things as we are, yet without sin. Therefore let us draw near with confidence to the throne of grace, so that we may receive mercy and find grace to help in time of need (Hebrews 4:15-16).

In my late thirties, God moved me cross-country away from my family and friends and all that I knew.

Prior to that move, I had never considered myself to be the touchy-feely type, but suddenly I found myself in an environment where I knew nobody, and in a culture where people were not apt to hug a stranger. After a number of weeks, I began to feel a real void. It was a new experience for me, this longing for touch.

I began to volunteer with this ministry that ran a prayer and healing room once a week and also collected clothes and supplies for people in need. On the appointed day, people from the surrounding communities would come to receive prayer and supplies.

One day, a young homeless mother came in with her baby. The visit wasn't her idea, so she was resistant and arrived with chip on her shoulder and her feet ready to run out the door.

When she walked into the prayer room, what I felt most was not God leading me in how to pray for her, but Him leading me to give her a big hug!

I walked up and put my arms around her, and immediately she broke down in tears. Collapsing onto the floor, she lay there for a couple hours just crying. When she got back up, she explained that she had been homeless for a few years, and it had been a really long time since anyone had hugged her, and that hug had broken through all of her defenses.

That day, I understood the void and pain she felt in a way I wouldn't have just a month or two prior. I couldn't help but think of my own struggles after just a few weeks of being away from my friends and family and was horrified at the thought of what it would feel like to go years without a hug as so many on the streets and in prison have to endure.

God knew that mother's greatest need that night was not prayers for a place to stay or a job, or diapers for her baby, but love given in the form of touch. He also knew that due to my recent experience, I would be equipped with the compassion to administer it.

If we will allow Him, God will use even the oddest of our circumstances for good. Like Jesus, who was tempted in all things and therefore is able to sympathize with our weaknesses and offer mercy and grace, we ourselves can step in and offer mercy and grace from that place of knowledge and compassion gained through our circumstance.

Prayer Focus

Father, let me see with higher vision and learn to waste nothing. Help me offer up to you my circumstances to be used for your glory. Let me be a willing vessel of compassion, mercy and grace.

Day 24- The Power of the Tongue

Let your speech always be with grace, as though seasoned with salt, so that you will know how you should respond to each person (Colossians 4:6).

Death and life are in the power of the tongue, And those who love it will eat its fruit (Proverbs 18:21).

When God spoke the Earth into existence so many years ago, those words of creation are still creating universes today. When He said, let there be light, light is still coming into existence!

There are few lessons that I believe are as monumental a game changer as the power of spoken words.

There is no mystery why God says so few words audibly. He fully knows the power behind each spoken word. And we are created in His image. When we are fully who we are in Christ, our words will carry the same ability as Christ's did.

Greater authority on our words is so slowly granted because God must be able to trust us to not speak haphazardly before He can give us real authority in that area. We want to be able to say, "mountain move" and the mountain to be moved. But until our lips cease speaking words that degrade, curse, and bring death, we cannot be entrusted with that kind of authority.

Our bad day, the past circumstances, the fact that the person deserved the curse words spoken, none of those things can play into the picture, and as long as they do, you disqualify yourself from greater authority on your words.

The power of life and death truly is in the tongue.

Prayer Focus

Father, help me to practice self-control and use my tongue to bring life instead of death.

Day 25- The Fire Season

For You have tried us, O God; You have refined us as silver is refined (Psalms 66:10).

The year I moved to California, there was a huge brushfire that burned a lot of Yosemite National Park and the surrounding areas.

But out of that fire was birthed an abundance of rare mushrooms called a Morel mushroom.

Mushrooms are actually a fruit, not a vegetable. And this fruit is valuable because it requires special conditions to grow. Morel mushrooms require not only the high heat of natural fire, but the decay of what has died in the fire, proper moisture, and the symbiotic relationship with its host environment to grow. It makes the fruit almost impossible to produce by any manmade means, which is what makes them so valuable.

Because of the high value of Morel mushrooms, some have even tried burning land to grow the mushrooms but have rarely had success.

After the fires in Yosemite, mushroom hunters started sneaking into the closed off areas of the park and risking their lives from falling trees and other dangers to search for this fruit. At the time, park rangers estimated that there was between 40 and 160 million dollars' worth of Morel mushrooms present in the park.

Through these events, God stirred my heart and said to me, do not despise the fire seasons of your life, for they can produce some of the most abundant and valuable fruit.

As people we sometimes go through prolonged seasons of fire, death, decay and loss. In those times, we must learn to stick close in a symbiotic relationship with Christ, surrendering that from the past which is now dead and letting Christ water us. If we will do this, new gifts and new life will be birthed from these harsh seasons, and the fruit will be of great value.

When you emerge from the fire, open your eyes to what has been birthed in and through you, lest it be taken from you in your unawareness.

Fire seasons do occur, but they do not have to be in vain. In fact, God desires to turn those fire seasons into that which produces much fruit and is of great value!

Prayer Focus

God, help me to not despise the fire seasons. Help me to recognize that what you are cultivating in me during those times is of great value.

Day 26- Enter into His Rest

By the seventh day God completed His work which He had done, and He rested on the seventh day from all His work which He had done. Then God blessed the seventh day and sanctified it, because in it He rested from all His work which God had created and made (Genesis 2:2-3).

So there remains a Sabbath rest for the people of God. For the one who has entered His rest has himself also rested from his works, as God did from His (Hebrews 4:9-10).

"Come to Me, all who are weary and heavy-laden, and I will give you rest. "Take My yoke upon you and learn from Me, for I am gentle and humble in heart, and YOU WILL FIND REST FOR YOUR SOULS. "For My yoke is easy and My burden is light" (Mathew 11:28-30).

There were many years of my life when I was stuck in this pattern of striving. I found myself regularly telling God how tired I was and that the efforts to live for Him were too much to keep up.

He began to tell me that He was going to teach me how to rest.

At first, I didn't understand. And, in my immaturity, I remember feeling disappointment because I thought that meant He didn't want to use me and was putting me on the shelf, which to me sounded like rejection.

I had a lot to learn about His heart! I didn't know that His primary motive is not to use us, or about what we can do for Him or us being good servants, but about love and relationship.

Love and relationship will lead us to co-labor beside Christ, not us laboring on our own for Christ.

There is a difference between working and striving. All work is not striving. Striving is working under your own or other people's power or yoke and not Christ's. In doing so, you work much harder than you were intended to.

We are to work with Him as sons and daughters of God. In this, we will receive His refreshing along the way. Our co-laboring will become a dance between work and rest, and no longer such a burden or obligation.

Over the years, I have come to realize that we actually labor for our own benefit, not His. Jesus doesn't need us to accomplish what He wants to accomplish, but it is His pleasure to work beside us.

God is Creator. He is Shepherd. He is Counselor and other aspects of work, and yet He also values rest. And when we step into who we truly are, we will also be a beautiful blend of both work and rest.

If you find yourself tired, weary, like you cannot go on, look for where you are laboring without Him, or where you are striving outside of rest.

Prayer Focus

God, show me where I am living from a place of striving instead of rest. Help me to trade my burdens and enter into your peaceful rest.

Day 27- Miraculous Rest

And He said, "My presence shall go with you, and I will give you rest" (Exodus 33:14).

Years ago, God gave me a prophetic picture about the miraculous power of his rest.

I was in Atlanta where there is this ten-mile stretch from the highway to where my parents used to live that has about twenty-five stoplights on it. On a good day, it takes about twenty-five minutes to get through the stretch, on a bad day about forty. Typically, you will have to stop at least momentarily at just about every light, and you feel like you've hit the jackpot if you can make it through more than two lights that are green.

But on this particular day, as I got about halfway down this stretch, I was in disbelief. Every light was green.

I started to think of the intersections in front of me and the heavy traffic and shopping areas and about how it was rush-hour on a Friday night. My mind was thinking there is no way I can make it all the way through this stretch on green lights! But I could feel a seed of excitement growing in me.

Not only did I make it down the entire ten-mile stretch without getting stopped by a single light, there were no yellow lights either. Every single light was fully green!

As I passed through many of the lights, I noticed the countdown numbers were all on six (a number often representing rest).

When I got through the end of the stretch, I looked down at my clock and noticed only six minutes had passed since I had exited the highway. Mathematically, it wasn't even possible in traffic or at the speed I was traveling. But that was God's point.

It is from the place of rest that the miraculous is accomplished. And the results of working from the rest of Christ will always be much more than what is possible through our own efforts and abilities.

Prayer Focus

God, help me to rest in You and see Your miraculous power!

Day 28- His Body

But now God has placed the members, each one of them, in the body, just as He desired. If they were all one member, where would the body be? But now there are many members, but one body (1 Corinthians 12:18-20).

For just as we have many members in one body and all the members do not have the same function, so we, who are many, are one body in Christ, and individually members one of another (Romans 12:4-5).

That they may all be one; even as You, Father, are in Me and I in You, that they also may be in Us, so that the world may believe that You sent Me. "The glory which You have given Me I have given to them, that they may be one, just as We are one; I in them and You in Me, that they may be perfected in unity, so that the world may know that You sent Me, and loved them, even as You have loved Me (John 17:21-23).

We live as part of Christ's body through the Spirit. It is a beautiful picture reflected in the makeup of our human bodies.

The human body is made up of an estimated 15 trillion cells. Each cell has a full measure of DNA and has contained within it everything it needs to develop into any body part.

Yet, despite the full complement of DNA making all functions a possibility, each cell develops according to a specific role and placement within the body. Likewise, God has placed us individually within the body of Christ in order for us to develop according to our call despite our physical ability to walk in other roles.

Just like the cells in our bodies, we reside in the wholeness of Christ. Each individual being is a small portion of His body, but His full DNA residing in each and every one of us. Making it truly us in Him and Him in us. This is also how it is possible to have the mind and the abilities of Christ and be one with Him.

In our human bodies, if the lung cells get sick, the entire body is affected. And if one cell gets displaced and goes rogue, it can become cancerous and spread and poison everything around it.

The negative impact of us functioning apart from our design or placement can also be seen within the body of Christ, making it all the more evident why the body can't function as it is truly meant to function until it is present in its entirety, healthy, in proper alignment, and functioning in corporate unity.

What a great privilege it is to be a part of Christ's body. May we never lose sight of that, or take it for granted. He includes us as a very part of who He is.

Prayer Focus

Jesus, help me to see Your people as part of one body and to better know and understand my role within that body.

Day 29- The Tension of the Gospel

"Peace I leave with you; My peace I give to you; not as the world gives do I give to you. Do not let your heart be troubled, nor let it be fearful" (John 14:27).

But the fruit of the Spirit is love, joy, peace, patience, kindness, goodness, faithfulness, gentleness, self-control; against such things there is no law (Galatians 5:22-23).

"These signs will accompany those who have believed: in My name they will cast out demons, they will speak with new tongues; they will pick up serpents, and if they drink any deadly poison, it will not hurt them; they will lay hands on the sick, and they will recover" (Mark 16:17-18).

We are made light to cast off darkness. We bring truth to dispel deception. We are peace to bring calm to chaos. We are love to counter hate. The gifts of the Spirit, and the entire gospel, are in themselves counter to the world in which we live.

Peace is not the absence of trials and storms. Peace is the calm and safety, even in the midst of the storms.

If we are thinking that having the fruit of the Spirit (love, joy, patience, peace, etc.) and walking in our calling will mean a quiet lifestyle, we are likely mistaken!

The fruit of the Spirit are weapons of warfare, not a means to living outside of tension.

Many want the peace and love and joy and miracles without their counter. But that will likely not be the reality in the natural world if we are going to preach the true gospel and be a light to the world.

The impact of light is only seen against a backdrop of darkness, and for the gospel to advance, there has to be a collision between darkness and light.

Christ lived the model Christian life and it was FULL of tension. His days consisted of false accusations of heresy, scandal over his choice of friends and lifestyle, the demon possessed, threats to his life in addition to the parts we like such as love, healing, and miracles.

Impact that remains is birthed out of the place of encounter where opposites collide and victory is made possible!

Do not fear the tension of the gospel. It is necessary and is the road to transformation!

Step forward, for you have been equipped, and Jesus has given you His peace!

Prayer Focus

God, help me to not lose sight that there is a war going on around us, or of the weapons I myself carry. Help me to go out into the darkness and shine my light.

Day 30- Glory to Glory

But we all, with unveiled face, beholding as in a mirror the glory of the Lord, are being transformed into the same image from glory to glory, just as from the Lord, the Spirit (2 Corinthians 3:18).

The LORD is my shepherd, I shall not want. He makes me lie down in green pastures; He leads me beside quiet waters. He restores my soul (Psalm 23:1-3).

I have often thought how life with God is kind of like a wave. You have the crest where everything is fast and furious in its intensity, and you feel like you can barely catch your breath. But then you have the gentle, sometimes monotonous lapping of low tide — the beginning point where things settle and the debris washes out before you gently get pulled back into the build of the next crest.

The thing is, a wave will cease to exist without low tide. And this is where the struggle is often found. People can get drawn into this perpetual state of trying to maintain the crest. They want to see the tangible glory, to be where things are thrilling and there is high visibility, accomplishment, and it's all about the fun. Many have come to fear the wave crashing to shore, the thrill dying down, the settlement and quiet where it seems like little is happening. But a rebuild is taking place.

This can lead people into a place where instead of going from glory to glory, they are holding tight and struggling to maintain yesterday's glory.

Ebb and flow are essential. The impurities and things that don't belong must be able to wash out in the quiet of low tide. And you must allow God to gradually strengthen and build you to sustain the next crest He is trying to build.

God is a God of work, and He is a God of rest. Both are essential to His being, and being created in His image, both are essential to ours.

Letting the wave come to shore and settle allows you to find a clarity and peace in the still waters that you couldn't find in the wave.

I have learned to value and embrace the still quiet of low tide. It is there that I best hear God's voice.

We cannot fear crashing to shore. Although jarring and unsettling in its nature, it just means that God is ready to start the build of the next wave that will take you higher than the one before.

Prayer Focus

God, help me to embrace the beauty of the process as you move me from glory to glory.

Day 31- The Heart of the Matter

"Blessed is the man who trusts in the LORD And whose trust is the LORD. "For he will be like a tree planted by the water, That extends its roots by a stream And will not fear when the heat comes; But its leaves will be green, And it will not be anxious in a year of drought Nor cease to yield fruit (Jeremiah 17:7-8).

One day God gave me a quick vision of a tree. What was unusual about it was that it was just the trunk of the tree, nothing else. This trunk was massive and heavily ribbed. It pulsated with life and expanded before my eyes.

I asked the Father about it, and He began to speak to me about the church, about how we often turn most of our focus onto the roots (biblical foundation), leaves and fruit (production, healing, miracles, etc.) of the tree, but ignore the very important trunk.

A top-heavy tree produces much foliage and fruit for the eyes, but it is prone to splitting and to falling over and uprooting the entire tree.

A bottom or root-heavy tree is susceptible to root rot from the stagnation of too much water and not enough air to breathe. Roots need oxygen to absorb and transport water. Otherwise, the very thing they are designed to carry will kill them.

Root rot cannot be seen without exposing the roots, but is often first suspected when the leaves of the tree begin to thin out and drop off. Then, people realize there is a deeper problem. Root rot is common in our church fellowships today, where one minute you see healthy thriving fellowships quickly turn to ones struggling to hold on.

God desires for there to be balance to the tree, for there to be a strong core or heart capable of transforming from the inside out. For it is the trunk or heart of the tree that makes possible transport and storage of nutrients, growth, strength, and protection from decay and predators. A healthy core (heart) is able to receive, able to give, and is better protected from disease and attack.

In nature, a tree whose trunk is bound does not mature and grow. It will eventually die, just as a bound heart grows cold and dies. Likewise, a tree whose trunk is not healthy quickly loses any water gained from the foundation or any energy gained from its leaves. Those resources, even in abundance, can't keep the tree alive.

But a strengthened core and transformed heart can both receive and distribute life giving water and sustain the energy of revival. These things are essential for the healthy church God is building. Will we allow Him to do the work and strengthen our core?

Prayer Focus

God, help us as a church to find healthy balance and to not just focus on what is most visible. Help us to thrive, carry and bring new life.

Day 32- Authentically You

Therefore let us draw near with confidence to the throne of grace, so that we may receive mercy and find grace to help in time of need (Hebrews 4:16).

In many ways, a relationship with God is similar to any relationship.

In the early stages, you are fearful of saying the wrong thing, acting the wrong way, being judged. You are thinking of what you can do to put your best foot forward, please that person, or show your affection.

In those beginning days you may act extra nice, possibly avoid certain topics to keep from sharing too much of what you really feel in case they disagree. You wonder if you should you buy them flowers, get your hair done special or buy a new outfit. There can be a lot of newness and mystery in this phase, but often neither person has really gotten to see the real person across from them.

Unfortunately, many people's relationship with God gets stuck in this new relationship phase. Some have been having a first date with Him for ten, thirty, fifty years and have never really gotten to know Him. Many are still spending time trying to hide from God what they are really feeling, trying to put their best foot forward and pretty it up in the name of being holy. Not realizing they were declared holy and set apart before they were even born.

We can live our lives never getting comfortable enough with God to know that the things we do to impress or prove our love are NOT the things most important to Him.

He is not looking for us to prove anything. He prefers that we be ourselves, the person He created us to be. He wants us to tell Him what we really feel, and to spend time with our real person. As with any relationship, it is the real authentic places that bring the deepest intimacy.

He truly invites you to come as you are and lay down your worry about appearances and expectations and let go of the new relationship pressure.

He invites you to come and not believe the lie that you are dishonoring Him by bringing your authentic self. That lie will keep you bound.

Prettied up and extra special is nice on occasion, but it can never compare to the authentic you. Dare today to be the real you with God. I promise you that you won't regret it!

Prayer Focus

God, give me the courage and confidence to draw near to You in intimacy and authenticity.

Day 33- Set Your Gaze

Then the LORD God called to the man, and said to him, "Where are you?" He said, "I heard the sound of You in the garden, and I was afraid because I was naked; so I hid myself." And He said, "Who told you that you were naked? Have you eaten from the tree of which I commanded you not to eat?" (Genesis 3:9-11).

Finally, brethren, whatever is true, whatever is honorable, whatever is right, whatever is pure, whatever is lovely, whatever is of good repute, if there is any excellence and if anything worthy of praise, dwell on these things (Philippians 4:8).

"Who told you that you were naked?" This was God's response to the fear that had risen up in Adam and Eve's heart, causing them to hide from Him.

God's words echo across all the fears and untruths in our lives. Who told you that you are stupid, who told you that you are ugly, who told you that you are a failure?

What voices are you listening to? What cry are you rallying around and allowing to penetrate your heart? If it is anything but what God has said about you and about your situation, then you are rallying around the wrong voice and have eaten from the wrong tree!

The enemy will always tell you that you are being short-changed, that you are limited by your weaknesses, that someone else is holding you back. But the eating and sharing of this fruit leads only to destruction and death.

Satan will tell you that you are naked and therefore vulnerable and needing to protect yourself, when God's truth is you are naked, beautifully free, under His protection and more than capable of rising above anything the enemy throws at you!

You become that which you continually gaze upon.

Before she ate of the bad fruit, Eve gazed upon it, she considered it, and the Bible says she saw it was a delight to the eyes. Bad fruit often has the appearance of something good, and Satan's lies always have some element of truth to them.

They were indeed naked, but that was not the prevailing truth or the final word on the matter.

Eating of bad fruit still brings death and destruction today, but God invites us to gaze upon the good fruit available to us.

Prayer Focus

God, help me to listen to the right voice, your voice, and be mindful of what I set my gaze upon.

Day 34- Room for Both

'For I know the plans that I have for you,' declares the LORD, 'plans for welfare and not for calamity to give you a future and a hope (Jeremiah 29:11).

Sometimes we have passions or giftings that may seem at odds with each other.

When we experience this, it can cause us to believe we must choose between those things or that if one is happening, the other can't. But that isn't always the case. Often, God has made room for both.

To speak to this, years ago God asked me to make a trip to the Reagan Presidential Library where He highlighted Reagan's journey to presidency.

Most people in the United States know about Ronald Reagan's acting career prior to him becoming president, but don't really know a lot of the details of the story.

God did not raise Reagan to presidency through the ranks of politics. He had a very different path. As a young man, Reagan's interests were high school and local theater which opened the door to broadcasting sports events. He later enlisted in the army, but couldn't go to war because of poor eyesight. I am sure this seemed like a discouraging defeat for him and likely gave no indication of where things were headed. But God was working His own plan.

The army knew about Reagan's history in theater and broadcasting and decided to put him to work making training videos for the military. This unexpected assignment opened doors for him not only with movies, but to be the face of and ambassador for General Electric where he got to go around the world listening to people's complaints and solving problems for GE. This would be God's training ground for foreign relations and public policy.

God didn't use politics to train up and open the door for Reagan, He used creative arts!

It reminds me of King David in the Bible, who went from harp player and shepherd to king. When God anointed David to become king, He did not call him to leave behind his heart of worship, or his heart to shepherd and lead a flock, but rather to carry those things with him into kingship.

To the human eye, your God-given passions and gifts may seem to be at odds with one another, but not to the Creator of the universe.

Be encouraged, have faith, and trust in what God has placed in your heart. You don't need to know how it will all fit and come together, just trust the One who does.

God is in the business of turning actors into presidents, musicians into kings, and tax-collectors into disciples. And through them, he works to change the world!

Prayer Focus

God, help me to not put limitations on myself that You did not set. Help me to trust You to guide me and pull all the pieces together.

Day 35- The New Thing

"Truly I say to you, whoever does not receive the kingdom of God like a child will not enter it at all" (Luke 18:17).

"For the earth will be filled With the knowledge of the glory of the LORD, As the waters cover the sea" (Habakkuk 2:14).

When I was a child, my family took a trip to Hawaii. During the first days of the trip, I found this little hermit crab out on the beach. Being the future biologist that I was, I took a clear plastic cup and a handful of sand and took him back to my hotel room with me.

My parents didn't say anything because they thought the crab would surely be dead by morning. But he wasn't, and I carried him around the islands with me for the week, intent on him being a permanent part of the family.

I remember getting to the airport and sticking that cup down into my bag and sending it down the security belt, nervous that crab was going to show up on the x-ray machine and security would not let me keep him. But he really was too small for that to be an issue.

I carried that crab all the way back to the mainland. Being a little kid, I knew absolutely nothing about taking care of hermit crabs. I knew nothing about the pH balance of salt water, or other things the crab might need.

I used my allowance to buy a small plastic fish tank to put him in and took some sand from my sandbox outside. I fed him lettuce because it was mentioned in the encyclopedia (that was our Internet of the day). My parents humored me, still waiting for the creature to drop dead.

But that little crab lived for years! I can't explain how, but he did.

One day the Holy Spirit brought that crab to remembrance. He said it was a message to me and the church for the harvest season.

He said many think that the move that has already begun is small, temporary and child's play. That the efforts and effects can never last because of inexperience and lack of resources. Many humor and many mock, but just like with that crab, will and determination will sustain the effort for years to come until He deems the season over.

God reminded me that day that we should not correlate the fact that we don't know what we are doing with our ability for success. The nature of a new thing is that no one will have experienced it before. But that won't hinder it from happening. He instructed that we use what we do know, and what we do have, and trust Him to multiply it into something that will last.

I have taken those words with me into many a new season.

Prayer Focus

God, help me to have faith like a child. To have the determination and strength to go the distance to see your glory cover the Earth.

Day 36- Goodness that Never Wanes

Or do you think lightly of the riches of His kindness and tolerance and patience, not knowing that the kindness of God leads you to repentance? (Romans 2:4).

"But I say to you, love your enemies and pray for those who persecute you, so that you may be sons of your Father who is in heaven; for He causes His sun to rise on the evil and the good, and sends rain on the righteous and the unrighteous" (Mathew 5:44-45).

God never stops loving and believing in us.

He never stops pouring out His goodness and blessing.

There is a part of us that wants to ask why would God give good things to this one or why would He promote that one. But that is the part of us that slides so easily back into the mentality that He treats us according to our works and deeds rather than according to His own goodness and irrevocable love.

The Bible tells us that God's kindness leads to our repentance. His kindness comes first, not the other way around.

If God's goodness ever waned, then a loss of hope in Him could be justified.

It is always good to remember that He causes His sun to rise on the evil and the good, and sends rain on the righteous and the unrighteous. This is unconditional love. And because His sun rises on evil like it does good, there is always hope for repentance and restored fellowship with Him.

It is the beauty of an eternal hope and eternal love that is only found within the person of Christ.

Prayer Focus

God, I thank you for your kindness and goodness, and for the plans you have for my life. Thank you that you never stop pouring out your love and blessings over us.

Day 37- Here Today

However, you are not in the flesh but in the Spirit, if indeed the Spirit of God dwells in you. But if anyone does not have the Spirit of Christ, he does not belong to Him. If Christ is in you, though the body is dead because of sin, yet the spirit is alive because of righteousness (Romans 8:9-10).

Religious leaders in Jesus' time had Him right in front of them, but didn't recognize Him as the Messiah because He did not come in the image or form they thought He would.

He didn't come dressed as a king and surround Himself with only those considered "worthy." He didn't point fingers and stone the sinners because of their sin. He just wasn't religious enough for their liking!

Today, many still believe Jesus and His followers should be ones to point fingers and condemn those who aren't "living right"; to only surround themselves by those who are "worthy" and who have the proper appearance of the religious.

Many, like the Pharisees of Jesus' day, still devote their lives to their own created image of the Messiah. All the while, they miss Jesus' true heart and purpose, to bring life and love and for us to be one family with Him, the Father and one another.

Jesus gave us His Spirit to live inside of us so that His presence would be with us on Earth. But millions of professed Christians have Him right there with them in the form of the Holy Spirit and don't recognize Him. They don't know or don't believe that He is truly present, that they can talk to Him and that He actually communicates back! Missing Him in spirit as He was once missed in body. They, like the religious leaders of the past, only look to the scriptures and miss enjoying life with and being discipled by the actual person.

Jesus is just as present today on earth as He was with his disciples thousands of years ago, and He still moves in power, does miracles, heals and delivers!

Prayer Focus

Jesus, thank You for your Spirit. I pray that eyes would be open to see You and recognize Your presence here on Earth.

Day 38- The Character of Christ

For those whom He foreknew, He also predestined to become conformed to the image of His Son, so that He would be the firstborn among many brethren (Romans 8:29).

Character is important because if you are not adopting the character of Christ, then you are not becoming like Him.

We should be mindful that character and behavior modification are not the same thing.

When you develop true character in Christ, you will be transformed, having adopted the nature of the One whom you are intimate with and it will be a permanent part of you. It will no longer be something that you can just easily decide to put on or take off.

People talk a lot about the importance of how you act, but acting is not the same as being. When you act, you temporarily put on a show the audience wants to see.

You can choose to act nice, act humble, act forgiving or any way you please through behavior modification without it ever being a part of who you are. When you do this, people may think you have good character by the characteristics you are showing them, but it could just be an act.

But the temporary and superficial nature of behavior modification lends itself to falling apart when pressure is applied and there is not a permanently transformed heart beneath that can stand as a foundation under the pressure.

Characteristics can be taught and acted out, but character is only achieved through a heart transformed.

Prayer Focus

God, transform my heart so that I may be conformed to the image of Your Son, Jesus Christ.

Day 39- The Open Casting Call

Brethren, I do not regard myself as having laid hold of it yet; but one thing I do: forgetting what lies behind and reaching forward to what lies ahead, I press on toward the goal for the prize of the upward call of God in Christ Jesus (Philippians 3:13-14).

One day I was lying in bed complaining to God about all the trials, hardship, betrayal and pain that seemed to have invaded my life. I asked Him, "God, who is in my corner?"

He did not directly address my laundry list of issues. Instead, He reminded me of the story of Joseph in the Bible and asked me who was in Joseph's corner when he was thrown into the pit, sold into slavery by his own brothers, lied upon and wrongly jailed for years?

You see, that anointing for big things is not free. And learning to overcome things that aren't fair or aren't easy, or require you, in seasons, to stand alone is part of growing into those kinds of anointings.

And they are grown into. You don't just wake up one day and find yourself ruler of Egypt without having first been prepared to walk in those shoes.

When a preacher stands at the front of the church talking about God raising up Daniels or Josephs or Esthers and releasing this or that anointing, everyone is quick to say, yes, yes, pick me! But then when God is like, ok, let's start that journey which may involve hardships like the pit or the jailhouse, reality quickly invades and suddenly, being the next Joseph or Esther takes on a new light.

Friends, a lot of times it is not about God picking you or not picking you for the job. It is about YOU saying yes, and then following through on walking through the process and paying the necessary cost.

Such invitations are open to all. God is forever offering the opportunity to step into powerful anointing like that of a Joseph, Daniel, or Esther. He just has very few takers for saying yes to go through the process necessary to walk in such high a calling.

We all want the anointing without having to pay the high price.

That morning God was not going to address my list of all that had gone wrong. His message to me was clear, you can choose to pay the price for a high calling or not. He won't baby us through it, for carrying such an anointing requires the highest of maturity!

It's an open casting call. Are we willing to say yes?

Prayer Focus

Father, I thank you that You prepare us for what You lead us into. Help me to embrace the journey and endure the preparation to become who You have called me to be.

Day 40- Inheriting the Nations

"And everyone who has left houses or brothers or sisters or father or mother or children or farms for My name's sake, will receive many times as much, and will inherit eternal life" (Mathew 19:29).

I will surely tell of the decree of the LORD: He said to Me, 'You are My Son, Today I have begotten You. Ask of Me, and I will surely give the nations as Your inheritance, And the very ends of the earth as Your possession' (Psalm 2:7-8).

When you choose to let go of family, home or worldly goods for the gospel, there is an exchange that happens. Your surrender of man's view and priorities allows you to begin to see the world and family through God's eternal viewpoint.

Suddenly, you wake up and realize the whole world is your family and everyone is your brother or mother or father or child, and you realize everywhere you go with God is home, not just the place you left behind.

In this monumental shift, you gain a hundredfold, and then some by the transformation of mind that allows you to think and see from an eternal perspective.

When you begin to treat the world like your own family, the world begins to treat you the same and they open up their hearts, homes and resources to you.

As with Christ, when you give yourself to the nations, the nations become your very inheritance.

Prayer Focus

God, give me Your heart for the nations. Help me to take on Your perspective and be stirred to ask You for my inheritance of the nations.

Day 41- The Position of the Heart

You younger men, likewise, be subject to your elders; and all of you, clothe yourselves with humility toward one another, for GOD IS OPPOSED TO THE PROUD, BUT GIVES GRACE TO THE HUMBLE. Therefore humble yourselves under the mighty hand of God, that He may exalt you at the proper time (1 Peter 5:5-6).

Humility is a position of heart. It is how you view yourself in relation to others.

Never talking about the things God has done for you because you don't want to APPEAR to not be humble is FALSE humility. True humility sees the value in the blessings you have been given no matter how small and thanks God for even what is yet to come.

Calling yourself unworthy or lowly may give the APPEARANCE of humility, but it is FALSE humility and also is a lie against the value God Himself placed on you and who He has created you to be.

A humble person knows exactly who they are, and the privileges they have been given, but still esteems their own importance to be no higher than that of anyone else.

There is no hierarchy in humility.

The truly humble will care nothing about self-reputation and will sacrifice reputation to give their lives for the very ones who will mock, scorn and not appreciate it in their own lack of humility. It is the paradox of humility.

The difference between humility and false humility will always be found in the heart, not in the eyes of those standing and judging from the outside. But fret not, God sees the true heart of man.

Prayer Focus

God, help me to walk in true humility, to lay down false images, and be rightly positioned in my heart.

Day 42- The Price of Intimacy

Now as they were traveling along, He entered a village; and a woman named Martha welcomed Him into her home. She had a sister called Mary, who was seated at the Lord's feet, listening to His word. But Martha was distracted with all her preparations; and she came up to Him and said, "Lord, do You not care that my sister has left me to do all the serving alone? Then tell her to help me." But the Lord answered and said to her, "Martha, Martha, you are worried and bothered about so many things; but only one thing is necessary, for Mary has chosen the good part, which shall not be taken away from her" (Luke 10:38-42).

If you are one who has high value for intimacy with Christ, there will be times when that value is questioned by those who don't hold it at as high a priority.

It reminds me of Luke Chapter 7 and the disciples' reaction to Mary pouring over Jesus the alabaster vial of perfume that cost the equivalent of a year's salary. Even those closest to Jesus accused her of wasting money that could have been spent on the poor, something they viewed as a more worthy cause than her focus of intimacy.

And later when Martha complained that her sister Mary was leaving her to do all the serving while she relaxed at Jesus' feet, Jesus' response was that "one thing is necessary," the same "one thing" that David spoke of when he said, *"One thing I have asked from the Lord, that I shall seek; That I may dwell in the house of the Lord all the days of my life to behold the beauty of the Lord and to meditate in His temple"* (Psalm 27:4).

In his writings, Jesus' disciple Luke termed Martha's focus on service a distraction. We often don't consider that service and good works can distract us from what is most necessary and beneficial.

But Jesus did not command that Martha give up her service and come join Mary at his feet. He never forces us into intimacy. He told her that she was worried and bothered by so many things and said that Mary had chosen the best part and it would not be taken from her.

I feel this is a promise given to each and every one of us. We are always free to remain or re-join the busyness of a life focused on service and work first, but while we continue to choose the best part, to focus on intimacy first, it will not be taken from us.

God will always answer our desire for more intimacy and make room for it.

Jesus chose to model intimacy and relationship first, with service being an overflow out of that. Putting things before intimacy will leave us weary, worried, and wanting of something more.

God invites us into greater intimacy, but we can anticipate that there will be push back from even those serving Him. Intimacy comes at a price. But intimacy results in the greatest relational reward – that we may behold the beauty of the Lord.

Prayer Focus

Jesus, thank You for Your invitation to intimacy. May we value it enough to pay the price of possibly being misunderstood or ridiculed.

Day 43- Prayer and Intercession

Since we have a great high priest who has passed through the heavens, Jesus the Son of God, let us hold fast our confession. For we do not have a high priest who cannot sympathize with our weaknesses, but One who has been tempted in all things as we are, yet without sin (Hebrews 4:14-15).

You have made them to be a kingdom and priests to our God; and they will reign upon the earth (Revelation 5:10).

There is a difference between prayer and intercession.

While every intercessor prays, not every prayer is one of intercession. In fact, the majority aren't. Why? Because intercessory prayers have been bought with a price and therefore carry a weight of authority that normal prayer does not.

When I say bought with a price, I mean there is sacrifice attached to that prayer. The person who prayed it has willingly made a choice to sacrifice on behalf of others. And what is done with a sacrifice but to light it aflame, to consume it as fuel to produce light and open the way for something much greater!

There is teaching in some church fellowships today that sacrifice is unnecessary because Christ paid the price and was the ultimate sacrifice and no others are required. To this, I both agree and disagree.

I wholeheartedly agree that no sacrifice is REQUIRED. Rest assured, you can be a believer in Christ having never sacrificed a thing and you will still be in Christ through your belief in Him. Your place in Christ is not in jeopardy. But to FOLLOW Christ is to follow Him to the cross and into a life of sacrificing for the freedom of others.

This is love, laying down our lives for others. And this was the whole objective of Christ's life on Earth, to show us how to love and receive the love of the Father! Where are we following Him to except to the cross? And how can He be our model if we are not modeling after Him?

Christ is our High Priest, and we are His priesthood. And the priest role has not changed. The one who steps into their priestly role will offer sacrifice and prayers of intercession. That is part of the role, always has been.

You can be a believer in Christ and never step into your priestly role of interceding for others. You can attend every church prayer meeting, call yourself an intercessor and be on the intercessory team, but never actually intercede if your altar of sacrifice is empty. Interceding is sitting in proxy and paying a cost for another.

Not everyone is willing to step into the priestly role because of the sacrifice and purity it demands. But those who do, still carry the power to bring great shifts and breakthrough, to do what most others can't or aren't willing to do.

In truth, part of our freedom in Christ is that we get to say no to things without threat of punishment or retribution. Live His life, or don't. It is up to us. But in this time when people are crying out to God for the restoration of power to the church, that power will come through consumption of sacrifice as we lay ourselves on the altar, are consumed and become ourselves a living sacrifice!

<u>Prayer Focus</u>

God, give me your heart for intercession, a heart willing to sacrifice for the wellbeing of others.

Day 44- A Heart for Intercession

Now the LORD saw, And it was displeasing in His sight that there was no justice. And He saw that there was no man, And was astonished that there was no one to intercede; Then His own arm brought salvation to Him, And His righteousness upheld Him (Isaiah 59:15-16).

For we do not have a high priest who cannot sympathize with our weaknesses, but One who has been tempted in all things as we are, yet without sin (Hebrews 4:15).

The words of Isaiah, that in all of Israel there was no one that would intercede, have always made me a bit sad. But as I have come to understand the price of true intercession, I have come to understand the plight.

To be able to intercede, one must be able to identify with the one whom they are interceding for. This is why Christ is able to intercede for us because He was tempted in all things, walked in our shoes, and was willing to pay the price to set captives free.

Years ago, while on a visit to California, I met a woman while at Angelus Temple. At the time, God was preparing both of us for a move to California.

In speaking to her, I found that she had a heart to help the homeless, and her plan was to move to Los Angeles and live amongst the homeless for a year or two before starting her ministry. She told me how she needed to be able to fully identify with their struggles. This was a picture of true intercession!

Today, God still looks to intercede through man. But often, there is no intercessor because few are willing to pay the cost of willingly putting themselves into the shoes of another to see their victory.

As God invites us into deeper levels of intercession, He also invites into a discussion over the costs.

How much are we willing to pay for other people's freedom, to see governments, cities and nations gain their victory? Because there is a cost. God never forces our hand. He lays out the cost, and you partner willingly or not at all.

God still prefers to work through man on this earth, so He still looks for intercessors willing to set captives free.

But while there is a high cost to intercession, there is also great privilege, honor and reward in heaven!

Prayer Focus

Jesus, give me your heart for intercession. Help me be one willing to stand in the gap for my fellow man.

Day 45- The Priest's Baptism

Then Jesus arrived from Galilee at the Jordan coming to John, to be baptized by him. But John tried to prevent Him, saying, "I have need to be baptized by You, and do You come to me?" But Jesus answering said to him, "Permit it at this time; for in this way it is fitting for us to fulfill all righteousness." Then he permitted Him (Mathew 3:13-15).

I believe one of the most overlooked or undervalued pictures in the western church is that of baptism.

When asked about baptism, many in the church will mention that it is a symbolic way to identify with the death and resurrection of Christ, which is a beautiful and powerful picture. But I believe there is so much our western culture misses or that we don't talk about when it comes to baptism.

Baptism by full immersion was required by Levitical law for consecration to the priesthood. This would occur at about thirty years of age.

The high priest, or one given the authority by order of birth, would baptize a new priest into their ministry. This is the picture we see with John the Baptist (whose father was high priest) baptizing Jesus at thirty years of age into his own ministry.

This was not because Jesus needed cleansing from his sins, as He was sinless. But in order for Jesus, by natural earthly standards, to have the role of priest conferred to Him, so that He could become our eternal High Priest to which He still stands. It was also necessary for the required cleansing of the sacrificial lamb by the priest.

If Jesus' baptism had not occurred, He would have usurped the natural order that is in agreement with Him being our High Priest and the sacrificial Lamb for the world's sin.

It is good to remember that Jesus did not come to abolish the Law, but to fulfill it.

For each of us, when we undergo baptism as a believer, it is also our priesthood that is being proclaimed, much more than just a symbolic gesture to identify with Jesus' death and resurrection.

Many ask if you need to be baptized for salvation, the answer is no. But baptism is a beautiful picture of your entryway into your God-given priestly role.

Prayer Focus

God, I thank you for baptism and the beautiful picture of who we are that it paints. May I not take for granted what you have made available to us.

Day 46- Memorial Stones

Jacob set up a pillar in the place where He had spoken with him, a pillar of stone, and he poured out a drink offering on it; he also poured oil on it. So Jacob named the place where God had spoken with him, Bethel (Genesis 35:14-15).

Until you settle in your heart that journeying with God requires faith, you will continually battle with a narrative that says that's not logical, that's just a story and couldn't have really happened.

There is plenty in the Bible, and in your walk with God, that you will never be able to put logic to because we see in part and know in part, and because God is so MUCH bigger than we are.

Faith is in the unseen and that which is not logical. If you could figure it all out and it all made sense without faith, then I would question if you were dealing with an all knowing, all powerful God at all.

Part of trusting God is trusting that what He tells you is true.

Be careful of letting other people's logic rob you and lead you out of faith. Trust the experiences God has given you and the miracles you yourself have seen!

The sharing of testimonies and memorial stones are important for those times when your logic wants to get in the way and cause you to downplay or rationalize what God did, or question what your spirit and experience knows to be true.

Keep your testimonies before you, for they bring encouragement in times of doubt and struggle.

Prayer Focus

God, help me to walk in faith and not in doubt. Help me in my times of struggle and doubt to remember how You have moved in my life in the past.

Day 47- Steadfast and Immovable

Wait for the LORD and keep His way, And He will exalt you to inherit the land (Psalm 37:34).

Therefore, my beloved brethren, be steadfast, immovable, always abounding in the work of the Lord, knowing that your toil is not in vain in the Lord (1 Corinthians 15:58).

What we choose to do during times of waiting and delay can make or break everything.

In 1 Samuel 13, the prophet Samuel told King Saul that he would come to him in seven days and to wait for him to come and show him what to do. But when seven days had passed and Samuel had not come, Saul took it upon himself to offer the sacrifice and prepare for war. This act of impatience and disobedience resulted in another man receiving the eternal kingdom instead of Saul.

God did not hold the prophet Samuel responsible for showing up late. Rather, He held Saul responsible for not continuing in obedience despite the delay.

Today, we often forfeit seeing God's kingdom established as we should because the moment we get the first sign that things may not occur on the expected timeline, we do like

Saul and turn to our own solutions and forfeit what God was working to establish.

But eternal things are outside of time and are not bound by earthly rules and expectations. We need to understand this so that we don't get hung up on the elements of time. Stay steadfast and immovable in your faith and see God do what He has promised!

Prayer Focus

God, help me to wait patiently on You, even when there seems to be delay. Help me to stay steadfast and not move in disobedience.

Day 48- Anchoring the Prophetic

"Before I formed you in the womb I knew you, And before you were born I consecrated you; I have appointed you a prophet to the nations" (Jeremiah 1:5).

"I will raise them up a Prophet from among their brethren, like unto thee, and will put my words in his mouth; and he shall speak unto them all that I shall command him" (Deuteronomy 18:18).

One of the tricky things about the prophetic is that it is subject to the vessel it flows through. This is why purity of heart is so incredibly important. I also think it is one of the reasons God will often show a prophet things out of season, sometimes years, decades or centuries ahead of time. Because in the heat of the moment, things have the potential to get skewed.

Our opinions, emotions, personal experiences, desires, political and theological views can all shape and alter how we interpret and deliver His word.

It is prudent to weigh carefully prophetic words, especially words spoken by overnight prophets. Those lacking years of experience and past grounding points to look back upon. Words given based only on where things are today with no grounding points from the past can be dangerous. They are like a tent with a single peg holding it down rather than one with many pegs to stabilize and secure it.

A prophet is not built in a six-week school or by a book or manual. Those things can be useful tools, but they won't come close to replacing years of history, hearing from, correction, and guidance from God.

Prayer Focus

God, purify the hearts of Your prophets, and let them be trustworthy and anchored fully in You.

Day 49- Tend Your Garden

And He spoke many things to them in parables, saying,
"Behold, the sower went out to sow; and as he sowed, some
seeds fell beside the road, and the birds came and ate them
up. Others fell on the rocky places, where they did not have
much soil; and immediately they sprang up, because they had
no depth of soil. But when the sun had risen, they were scorched;
and because they had no root, they withered away. Others fell
among the thorns, and the thorns came up and choked them
out. And others fell on the good soil and yielded a crop, some a
hundredfold, some sixty, and some thirty. He who has ears, let
him hear" (Mathew 13:3-9).

The word of God is a beautiful gift, whether it is the written
Word of God or a spoken prophetic utterance.

If we allow Him, God will use living prophetic words in
the same way He uses living scripture. He will show you
different things about them and focus attention toward the
words that address the place you are in at the moment.

But just like with scripture, if you never read what was
spoken, or mediate on it and reflect back, the words are
forgotten and do you little good.

Prophetic words are seeds. Seeds that must be put into
soil, watered and nurtured. If you get words and never do

anything with them, they become like seeds spilled on the ground that get washed away at the first rain, never taking root or growing into anything. We sometimes blame the prophet or God for the word not coming to pass, when it was lack of stewardship on our part.

It is our responsibility to receive God's word and nurture it. God partners with us. He doesn't do it all for us. We must tend our gardens!

On my journey, through the years, I have recorded hundreds of prophetic words and dreams in a journal. As I grow and learn, God constantly takes me back to those words to give me direction, reveal new things about them or has me look back to see and be encouraged.

And I have found that the better I steward the words He has given me, the more words He gives.

Value the beautiful gift of the Word of God.

Prayer Focus

Thank you, God, for your beautiful Word, both written and spoken. Let me value it and steward it well.

Day 50- The Governor Switch

"He who receives you receives Me, and he who receives Me receives Him who sent Me. He who receives a prophet in the name of a prophet shall receive a prophet's reward; and he who receives a righteous man in the name of a righteous man shall receive a righteous man's reward" (Mathew 10:40-41).

I have learned in my journey with God that the words and power of God have an almost built-in governor switch on them where things turn off when certain conditions are present.

Jesus teaches us that whoever welcomes a prophet as a prophet will receive a prophet's reward. And in the Bible, we see that Jesus was able to do few miracles in His hometown. Not because something was wrong with Jesus, or His authority was any less in His hometown. The people didn't believe in Him, and this worked like a self-limiting governor switch in their life.

There will be many in life who won't believe in you or your gifts, and they will not be able to receive from you because of that. As we mature, we need to learn to accept this and let people's receipt or rejection of us be its own determining factor.

In our human nature, we have a tendency to want to withhold from those who devalue us, treat us poorly, or themselves withhold from us. I will admit that at times I have been guilty of asking God, "why should I waste my time sharing the prophetic words or insights You have given me with someone who doesn't believe them?" But that's a bad attitude, and God has rebuked me at times for staying silent where I should have spoken.

We don't get to choose to withhold God's word or not minister to who He is calling us to minister. We don't get to be the determining factor on what words go out and who in turn will be blessed by them. And that goes for any of our gifts.

God has already built in His own measures to deal with hearts that aren't right, or positioned to receive.

It is our job to say what He says to say, do what He says to do, and not worry about the results and who receives from us and who does not. This can be hard when we feel rejected or like everything is falling on deaf ears. But God does not function based on merit, but on His goodness. And if we are going to represent Him and do His work, neither can we.

God makes available to all His goodness, but often people receive according to their own measuring sticks. This puts the limitations in their own hands, not God's and definitely not ours!

Prayer Focus

God, help me to believe Your word and workings and honor the righteous who minister.

Day 51- Beyond Disappointment

So when they had finished breakfast, Jesus said to Simon Peter, "Simon, son of John, do you love Me more than these?" He said to Him, "Yes, Lord; You know that I love You." He said to him, "Tend My lambs" (John 21:15).

Life comes with many disappointments. Having your expectations of someone disappointed is part of relationship and intimacy, even your relationship with God.

This could be seen even with Jesus' closest disciples. They thought they knew who He was, believing that He was coming to be a much different king, a king who would conquer and rule in the fashion they had always known a king to rule. But Jesus did not come with sword in hand ready to destroy all their enemies like they thought, and they had to learn who He was and adjust THEIR thinking to match HIS ways.

While God never fails in His objectives or in His love for us, disappointment will be part of the equation because disappointment is based on human expectation.

We, in our human minds, think we know the mind of God and how He will do things, but our thinking is earthbound, time-locked, and short-sighted. It is based on our experience, our temporary circumstances, our limited knowledge based from our little corner of the world. But God's actions will be based on the eternal objectives, the bigger picture and the final outcome.

You will not walk with Him without having times of disappointment when your expectations of how He will act aren't met. He does not fault us for our disappointment. But, in those moments, we must answer the question: Do we still love Him, and will we trust His love for us?

Sometimes when things crumble, you loving Him and Him loving you is all there is to hang onto. It gives meaning to the proclamation that love does not fail.

You may be doubtful of much, confused, angry, disappointed, disillusioned, but still, and sometimes to your surprise, the love remains.

Prayer Focus

God, help me to look beyond my disappointments in life and remember Your steadfast love.

Day 52- Promises of the Generations

But do not let this one fact escape your notice, beloved, that with the Lord one day is like a thousand years, and a thousand years like one day. The Lord is not slow about His promise, as some count slowness, but is patient toward you, not wishing for any to perish but for all to come to repentance (2 Peter 3:8-9).

It is often easy to forget that with God a day is like a thousand years and a thousand years like a day. It is also easy to forget that the promises of God are for the generations and not just for OUR current generation.

For a couple thousand years, the prophets spoke of redemption through a Savior that many generations died waiting to see. Yet those words of promise were still proclaimed over and over again across the generations.

There are times and seasons where the promises of God are often repeated and re-established. Rejoice in this. Do not grow weary and let your hearts grow hard toward the word of the Lord just because you have heard the same promises many times before and have yet to see them fulfilled.

There are many things we are seeing fulfilled today that the generations before us contended for but did not see, and there are many things we are contending for that will not be seen until future generations. This is part of us all being one and all being a part of the same story. You hold the hand behind you, and you hold the hand in front.

We can grow weary of hearing talk about revival when we see no evidence of deliverance that is still to come. Yet we still need to believe and contend for it, if not for our generation, then for the generations to come.

That is how the kingdom of God is advanced.

When I think of promises, I often think of Moses' story in the book of Numbers and how he responded. After years of trying to lead the Israelites into their land of promise, Moses found out he would die without seeing that fulfilment himself. But I love his response. He then turned and commissioned Joshua to take over the charge and told him that he would be with him. What a powerful picture of unity, timelessness, and of what our response is to be toward God's promises!

We cannot fall prey to disappointment over what hasn't happened yet, or into the trap of being self-centered, short-sighted or naïve. Cynicism can creep in when we hear the same promise repeated time and time again without fulfillment. But God knows the appointed time and has no issue with releasing a proclamation over and over until it is received.

Whatever promises God has spoken over you, believe for them this year and believe the next! We should rejoice in

God's reminder of His promises for things still available and waiting to be fulfilled. Those promises remain true whether we see them this year, years down the road, or in the generation to come!

Prayer Focus

God, help me where I struggle to believe for Your promises. Let me rest in your faithfulness to the generations.

Day 53- The Power of Kindness

But do you suppose this, O man, when you pass judgment on those who practice such things and do the same yourself, that you will escape the judgment of God? Or do you think lightly of the riches of His kindness and tolerance and patience, not knowing that the kindness of God leads you to repentance? (Romans 2:3-4).

Kindness is a heart response and a reflection of the high value you hold for another. As such, it speaks to the depths of the heart of the recipient.

True kindness is freely given and shows in a tangible way that you believe that person is worthy of that which you weren't mandated to give. This is why it is the kindness of God that leads people to repentance, because it speaks to the very core of who a person is and says 'you, just as you are, are worthy of my attention and effort.' This cuts through barriers like no sermon ever could.

When a person looks upon their own worth reflected through the actions of another, they are stirred to respond and actually moved to be that person of worth that was proclaimed through the freely given acts of the heart.

We struggle to grasp the power of genuine kindness, but kindness is a hallmark of those who have the greatest transformational impact.

Prayer Focus

God, give me a greater revelation of the power of kindness.

Day 54- The Pure Heart

Create in me a clean heart, O God, And renew a steadfast spirit within me (Psalm 51:10).

Moreover, I will give you a new heart and put a new spirit within you; and I will remove the heart of stone from your flesh and give you a heart of flesh (Ezekiel 36:26).

We live in a world that encourages us to choose according to our desires and following our heart. This is not necessarily wrong, but there can be a HUGE caveat to it.

How submitted to God and open is your heart? How covered over or wounded is it by past hurts and experiences? If you are talking about following a heart that is wounded, protected by walls and not fully open to the Father, then following your heart can get you into a lot of trouble!

A wounded or closed heart will often choose the safest, least painful, easiest and quickest way of obtaining what we want, and choose based on current circumstances and limited view alone. This may be a very different choice than what God would want for you.

God will honor the choices we make. He will bless us if we choose to spend forty years circling the desert because of the things we can't let go of, or if we choose a better way the first time.

Don't mistake His blessings and provision as a sign that you are on the path He would have chosen for you because a good Father will bless and provide for His children even in their wrong choices, obstinance and rebellion all the while patiently nudging us toward small course corrections in the direction we need to go.

As long as we have wounded and protected places in our hearts, we should walk with caution on the advice to just follow our desires and heart.

The good news is, God can use even our wrong choices as steppingstones to get us to where we need to go. So, in a lot of ways, it is fail-proof. But on some paths, we will spend a lot more time in fruitless places, toiling for no gain, and trudging through the desert!

As men, we often don't know our own heart, we ourselves have to learn what is in its depths that has never been uncovered or allowed to surface.

As our Father, God cares very much about our desires and the things of our heart and wants to give us those things. He also cares about our growth into fullness and about our protection and knows what is going to fashion us best into who He created us to be. Ultimately that is what will bring us the most joy and fulfillment.

As we mature and walk in health, we come to the place where we can trust and follow our hearts. But that happens through the process.

When your heart is abandoned and fully open to the Father, your will and His will become the same and the heart will be trustworthy. Then you will find yourself often foregoing the easier or the pain-free path, or the one that looks the most appealing in favor of the one that will bring ultimate life.

Prayer Focus

Purify my heart, God, and keep it tender and open to You.

Day 55- The Nature of the Cross

And those passing by were hurling abuse at Him, wagging their heads and saying, "You who are going to destroy the temple and rebuild it in three days, save Yourself! If You are the Son of God, come down from the cross" (Mathew 27:39-40).

The place of transparency and vulnerability is one of the most misunderstood positions one can subject themselves to.

It is no different for us than it was for Jesus. People see your wounds bared, they see you bleed and they usually liken it to weakness rather than to the fact that your ability to bleed and to bear scars and wounds speaks to your very humanity. A humanity we all share, no matter how strong or weak.

Jesus made a choice to put Himself in a position of vulnerability. He had the power to come down off that very visible cross, but didn't. Instead, He opened himself up to judgment, ridicule, misunderstanding and even pity. That is vulnerability.

But those who choose vulnerability know what many others don't. Exposure of all that you are, including your wounds and scars, is what allows others to identify with your humanity. Vulnerability also frees us from the trap of things like shame, guilt, and secrecy and brings the openness and freedom necessary for abundant life.

When you follow Christ, He will lead you to bare all and step with Him into the darkness and the woundedness of man. Why? Because when you rise from that place of darkness and death that everyone witnessed you in, you bring them with you into your hope, into your resurrection and into your victory and you let them know that such victory is also available to them.

When we bear our wounds and share our process of redemption, we invite others into the wonder of the very vulnerable, but beautiful nature of the cross.

Prayer Focus

God, help me to not be afraid to be vulnerable before You and before others.

Day 56- Good News

For Christ also died for sins once for all, the just for the unjust, so that He might bring us to God, having been put to death in the flesh, but made alive in the spirit (1 Peter 3:18).

He made Him who knew no sin to be sin on our behalf, so that we might become the righteousness of God in Him (2 Corinthians 5:21).

To the Jews I became as a Jew, so that I might win Jews; to those who are under the Law, as under the Law though not being myself under the Law, so that I might win those who are under the Law; to those who are without law, as without law, though not being without the law of God but under the law of Christ, so that I might win those who are without law. To the weak I became weak, that I might win the weak; I have become all things to all men, so that I may by all means save some. I do all things for the sake of the gospel, so that I may become a fellow partaker of it (1 Corinthians 9:20-23).

When I returned to the business world after years of being away, I was reminded of the harsh reality that how we are dressed will often determine who will associate with us.

Suddenly all the businessmen who had for years ignored me in my casual shirt and jeans would strike up a conversation as if my clothes alone announced that I had a brain in my head and could hold a meaningful conversation.

I wanted to be bothered by this because things like dress should not determine so much about how people view you. But this is how the world associates. If you look like an athlete, athletes will wave and talk to you. If you are dressed like a businessman, the business world will address you. If you are in your Sunday's best, people in the church will respect you. It is the reality of our world, and probably the reason why the Apostle Paul spoke of becoming all things to all men.

We like to think that all people should accept us in whatever package we present, and that drives talk about inclusion. But does it really hold water in the world? The reality is, people like to associate with those who are like them.

I believe that it is only in Christ that there is true inclusion for all. And not the Christ that many Christians present when they say, if you will come to our church, think like we think, talk like we talk, then we will call you Christian. But the Christ who looked down from the cross with thieves on either side, and a mob cheering on His death and still made a plea and voiced the words that included all.

Forgive them, for they know not what they do.

Christ's forgiveness covered the thieves. It covered those who drove the nails through his hands. It covered the government. It covered those who had abandoned him. And it covered the few who endured to follow him to the foot of the cross.

The world is hungry for inclusion. But, still today, it is only found within the heart of Christ.

May we return back to the true gospel where through Christ there is forgiveness and redemption that includes all. That is truly GOOD NEWS!

Prayer Focus

Jesus, thank You that You came for all and offer life to all.

Day 57 - Redemption of the Heart

"Then I will make up to you for the years that the swarming locust has eaten, the creeping locust, the stripping locust and the gnawing locust, My great army which I sent among you. You will have plenty to eat and be satisfied, And praise the name of the LORD your God, Who has dealt wondrously with you; Then My people will never be put to shame" (Joel 2:25-26).

O Israel, hope in the LORD; For with the LORD there is lovingkindness, And with Him is abundant redemption (Psalm 130:7).

God loves to redeem our "I'll nevers" in life.

I'll never live in this place; I'll never work that job; I'll never be like that person; I'll never marry someone like that.

Why? Because, like a mirror, those statements reveal the places where our hearts are closed to love, whether that be due to ignorance, misunderstanding, past pain or pride. God does not force Himself upon us, so those places where we are closed to love are the places where He, as love, will not inhabit until we give permission.

Over the years, He has sent me to live in numerous places on my "I'll never" list. And at first, I was like, "But you

KNOW how I feel about that place!" Which of course He did know and that was exactly why I found myself going.

But the result was that I came to love and have His heart for those cities.

When God gives us what we say we don't want, it is not out of spite, punishment, or withholding good things. Rather, it is often about redemption and us experiencing more of His heart and seeing through His eyes.

Sometimes what looks like nothing more than a piece of coal at first glance is actually a diamond!

Prayer Focus

God, help me to identify the places where I have built barriers to love. Help me to surrender those spaces so that love will have free reign in my life.

Day 58- The Power of Love

But now faith, hope, love, abide these three; but the greatest of these is love (1 Corinthians 13:1).

We have come to know and have believed the love which God has for us. God is love, and the one who abides in love abides in God, and God abides in him (1 John 4:16).

Years ago, I had an unusual experience. I got on the elevator to leave my apartment building and when the doors closed, I suddenly smelled the overwhelming scent of moth balls.

It was 5:15 in the morning so there weren't a lot of people who would be in and out of the elevator. And moth balls are rarely used today in the US because their purpose was to keep moths away that will destroy clothing and other materials. In our modern closets and homes in the US, this isn't typically a problem anymore, so moth balls are rarely found. But it was a smell I remembered from childhood.

I looked around the elevator and of course saw no signs of the offending item. But the smell was so strong that it made my eyes water.

The following night I was at a church and during worship my senses were again assaulted by the overpowering scent of moth balls, causing my eyes to water. I was pretty sure no one carried a package of moth balls with them to church, so I began to ask God what it was about.

I remembered back to the last encounter I had with moth balls. It was years before during bible college when my Korean roommate decided to put a few moth balls in one of her clothes drawers before leaving for the weekend, simply because she liked the smell and it reminded her of home.

Buried under a mound of clothes within her drawer, the moth balls weren't even open to the room and still they wreaked havoc!

My spending one night with those few moth balls in our small enclosed apartment resulted in burned nasal and throat passages and weeks of respiratory distress and asthma attacks. I had to move apartments for almost a week until it could be aired out enough that it didn't cause me coughing fits. I was well acquainted with the power of moth balls.

After church that night, God woke me up to talk about those moth balls. He told me the moth balls were a picture of the strength of impact that He intends his people have. The kind impact where one or two of them in a room would so permeate the atmosphere that it would ward off that which destroys and decays.

That is the raw power of God's love. To the enemy, love works like moth balls. It is offensive to the nose. It won't be ignored. It won't be hidden away. It reaches further, impacts stronger, and lasts longer than imagined!

We greatly underestimate the power of God's love, but I believe that in the coming days, we are going to see a greater manifestation of His love that, when unleashed, will shift atmospheres and change regions!

Prayer Focus

God, help me to come into a full realization of the great power of Your love and the impact it can have in the world.

Day 59- The Native Call of Home

"In My Father's house are many dwelling places; if it were not so, I would have told you; for I go to prepare a place for you. If I go and prepare a place for you, I will come again and receive you to Myself, that where I am, there you may be also. And you know the way where I am going" (John 14:2-4).

For here we do not have a lasting city, but we are seeking the city which is to come. Through Him then, let us continually offer up a sacrifice of praise to God, that is, the fruit of lips that give thanks to His name (Hebrews 13:14-15).

When I lived in Pasadena, California, I used to have many tropical parrots that lived in the trees around my house. These parrots are not native to Southern California, but the population has grown and spread over the years, and the city has become known for them.

The parrots love the rare mornings when it was rainy and the weather closely resembles the tropics. On those days, they are super vocal.

Most of the parrots in Pasadena today were born there, with probably only a few of them left having been the ones taken from the rainforest or held in captivity before they were freed by fire. But the natural inclinations of the rainforest are still there inside them, written upon their DNA, and passed from generation to generation.

I'm not sure that any of them will ever be taken back to their native land. I imagine that if they were, they would be in awe to finally find home and understand why the tropical weather has meant so much, and to know what if finally feels like to be cloaked in the depths of the rainforest. To discover that they aren't a community of hundreds as they thought, but belong to a company much greater.

It is the native land calling to the native.

One day we will all know that feeling when we are returned home to the One who created us and finally understand so much about us that remains a mystery while we are here on Earth. When we are surrounded by a multitude that are like us and fully cloaked in the depths of His glory.

Earth is not our home; this is a foreign land for each and every one of us. Our native land calls out to us. It is the Father beckoning us to return to Him.

The good news is we don't have to wait to get to know Him. We can know the Father through His Son Jesus, and begin to discover what is written on our DNA that has been passed through the generations. It is through them that we will really discover who we are and come into our being.

Prayer Focus

Father, draw me close to You. Help me to discover who I am in you, and all that you have written on my DNA.

Day 60- Heavenly Foundations

So then you are no longer strangers and aliens, but you are fellow citizens with the saints, and are of God's household, having been built on the foundation of the apostles and prophets, Christ Jesus Himself being the corner stone (Ephesians 2:19-20).

The height that a mountain can reach is determined by the strength of its foundation.

Mountains break off under the gravitational pull and opposing forces of nature once they reach the maximum that their foundation can support. But then we have mountains like Mount Everest which has endured for generations, and is the highest mountain in the world because of the strength of its base.

Every year in Spain, they hold a competition where they build what are called Castells, human towers. These towers can reach ten stories or more and are built solely of human bodies. But what the teams have learned over the years is that to go higher, they must find ways to build stronger at the base of the tower, sometimes packing in hundreds of bodies at the bottom layer to provide strength for the tower.

It has always been the dividing or weakening of a foundation that causes a fall and limits growth.

When a mountain is being formed, its peak is pushed up out of its foundation. While the peak might get all the glory, it is not the strength and true power of the structure. That lies at the foundation.

If we build the church upon the principle of focusing on the top of the mountain, we will build a church that won't be able to carry weight or burden and will crumble away over time. A stable church has a foundation of apostles and prophets, not for them to be showpieces. They are raised to be capable of carrying a high burden of weight and to be able to support and push others up from their foundation.

If we are looking to restore stability in the church, we must turn our focus to restoring proper foundations.

Prayer Focus

Jesus, help us to build and strengthen Your church. Restore proper foundation that will last through the generations.

Day 61- Walking in Authority

For the grace of God has appeared, bringing salvation to all men, instructing us to deny ungodliness and worldly desires and to live sensibly, righteously and godly in the present age, looking for the blessed hope and the appearing of the glory of our great God and Savior, Christ Jesus, who gave Himself for us to redeem us from every lawless deed, and to purify for Himself a people for His own possession, zealous for good deeds. These things speak and exhort and reprove with all authority. Let no one disregard you (Titus 2:11-15).

One walking in authority must work from a place of relationship or they will risk trampling and devastating those in their path. But authority is a funny thing. Spiritual authority will often trump natural or positional authority, and spiritual authority is subject to the carrier's knowledge of, identification with, and handling of that authority.

With authority comes much responsibility in how you use it. And the more you become grounded in your identity, the more you have to remember that.

God does not give us authority to dominate or become a dictator or to rise to places He is not leading us to rise to. Rather, I often see that the ones He has given the most authority to are the ones He knows are least likely to exert it unless they need to.

Authority has always been meant to be foundational, foundations supports without overtaking.

One of the reasons I often won't minister in a place where I have not built relationship is because the relationship adds in sort of a checks and balances system. I will be careful not to trample or exert authority where I shouldn't with those that I care about. I will protect their hearts. But without relationship, people's hearts can easily become casualties.

With authority, you won't avoid all hurt feelings, especially in top-down hierarchal systems where people may struggle with someone of a lesser title or who is not well-known stepping into the mix and moving in authority. God's authority doesn't always match man's opinion of who should be in the lead. But when God gives you authority and tells you to move, He will back you in that endeavor. So go forth with confidence and in your authority!

Prayer Focus

God, help me to be a good steward of the authority You have given me. Help me to step forward in confidence.

Day 62- Rightly Positioned

"Whoever exalts himself shall be humbled; and whoever humbles himself shall be exalted" (Mathew 23:12).

"Do not call to mind the former things, Or ponder things of the past. "Behold, I will do something new, Now it will spring forth; Will you not be aware of it? I will even make a roadway in the wilderness, Rivers in the desert" (Isaiah 43:18-19).

As you wait for God to open the promised doors, remember that humility is the position of entry.

Pride that won't allow you to go low can keep you from entering into the places God has for you.

Ancient doors were more like tent flaps or low entryways that required you to bow down to enter. When we are inflexible, unwilling to surrender our stance, or allow ourselves to be in a position that may appear to be one of weakness, we lessen our access to new places.

The change of position needed to cross over is typically short-lived. You bow on entry and you bow on exit, but it does require you to bend.

We sometimes want to go through the doors of life standing tall with all our baggage and stuff from the season we are supposedly leaving behind, but with God, rarely does it happen that way.

You have to let go of the old to take hold of the new. You have to bow down to then be brought higher.

Prayer Focus

Father, I give you permission to re-position me. Help me to let go of anything that will hinder forward movement.

Day 63- Weakness into Strength

And He has said to me, "My grace is sufficient for you, for power is perfected in weakness." Most gladly, therefore, I will rather boast about my weaknesses, so that the power of Christ may dwell in me (2 Corinthians 12:9).

Your weaknesses are often a reverse reflection of your true gifts.

Fearful Gideon hid out in the cistern, but his true nature was a man of great courage.

Moses, who stuttered, would later speak words that would alter the reality for the Israelites.

The Apostle Paul, whose overzealous passion was strong enough to turn him into a murderer, would make him one of the most passionate followers of Christ, bringing life instead of death.

Peter, who turned away in denial, would later stand bold as a lion and unmovable.

Have you ever wondered why Jesus would put a known thief in charge of the money as he did with Judas? Not because He was naïve or a negligent leader. I believe He saw in Judas the potential to overcome that weakness and make his money savvy a strength.

Part of growing into who you are created to be is learning to find the pearl in the oyster of your weaknesses, taking what man often labels as bad and turning it for good.

Learn to look upon your weaknesses not as such, but rather as the undeveloped precursor to what God is going to redeem.

See your weaknesses with new eyes because when partnered with Christ, they will be your strength!

Prayer Focus

God, help me to not be discouraged by my weaknesses, but rather to turn them over to You in order that they become my strength.

Day 64- Love Among Us

And the Word became flesh, and dwelt among us, and we saw His glory, glory as of the only begotten from the Father, full of grace and truth (John 1:14).

And He said to them, "Go into all the world and preach the gospel to all creation" (Mark 16:15).

Jesus could have charged his disciples to pray for the world and they all could have just camped out in comfort. After all, prayer is a powerful thing.

Instead, He told them to GO into all the world just as He came into ours.

I believe that is because you cannot change the heart of what you yourself don't love, and you cannot show love, know or be known from a distance. This is where we often miss it.

True love is best seen in the trenches where you really get to see who is for you and beside you versus who just says they are. I will believe the heart and the word of the person in the trench with me over the person at a distance every time!

Anyone can speak or prophesy, but do they hold the keys to transformation, which is always value and love witnessed in the flesh?

If your heart is to follow Christ, you will find yourself compelled to put flesh on that love and dwell among them as He came to dwell among us.

Prayer Focus

God, give me Your heart to go out into the world and share Your love.

Day 65- Running the Race

Therefore, since we have so great a cloud of witnesses surrounding us, let us also lay aside every encumbrance and the sin which so easily entangles us, and let us run with endurance the race that is set before us, fixing our eyes on Jesus, the author and perfecter of faith, who for the joy set before Him endured the cross, despising the shame, and has sat down at the right hand of the throne of God (Hebrews 12:1-2).

With their eyes set to the finish line, the runner of a relay race puts in their all, carrying the promise for their length of the journey.

In a relay race, everyone does not get to be the one to cross the end finish line, but each one who carries the baton is just as significant to the outcome of the race.

As a runner, we carry the baton as fast and hard as we can for the length we are meant to carry it, fully believing for the victory. When our energy is at its last and we are gasping for breath, we pass the baton to the next runner who is fresh to the race and energized to carry it the next leg. On some races, we may even run multiple legs of the race.

But as a good runner, we have to know when it is time to let go and pass the baton to the next runner.

In the races of life, we often view ourselves as a solo runner and operate under the assumption that we will run each race to the end point and carry the baton the entire length of the journey. We may feel like we failed when we reach the end of our endurance and must let go and pass the baton on without having crossed the line we thought we would cross.

But it is not failure to pass the baton to the next runner, and this is how the kingdom of God advances from generation to generation involving us all in this great race that spans the generations.

In the races we run, we are typically blinded to the true finish line, not knowing if we will be the one to carry the baton across, or one who will pass it along. But the victory belongs to all who ran in the race!

Prayer Focus

God, give me strength to run the race You have set before me, and to have the wisdom to know when it is time to pass the baton.

Day 66- Treasury of Testimonies

"This gospel of the kingdom shall be preached in the whole world as a testimony to all the nations, and then the end will come" (Mathew 24:14).

And they overcame him because of the blood of the Lamb and because of the word of their testimony, and they did not love their life even when faced with death (Revelation 12:11).

I have come to believe that just like with people, God has given each nation gifts and aspects of Himself to display. It is my favorite thing about traveling to new nations, the revealing of those aspects of God and the invitation the Father gives to claim those aspects as my own inheritance.

One night I had dream where I was in this gallery that had all these pieces of art and treasures from around the world. There were many people touring the gallery, but I was showing this one man items from the private stash of my collection.

As I opened the treasure boxes from each nation, there were these carvings of the faces of Jesus. And of all the art in the gallery, this is what interested the man the most. This surprised me on some level because he actually was not a believer in Christ, and I figured that would be what he was least interested in. But as he oohed and aahed and ran his fingers over the carved faces of Jesus, I began to focus on those and pulled out different ones to tell him about.

We often have expectations of who will receive what we have to share. But the more we get to know God, and begin display the hidden away faces of Him as individuals or as nations, the more we will see just how attractive the true faces of God are to even the biggest of skeptics!

We must dare to open up and share our personal treasures. The world is desperate to see God like they have never seen or heard of Him before, shared through our own testimonies.

Our testimonies are powerful tools for reaching the lost and overcoming the enemy. May we never underestimate their power!

Prayer Focus

God, give me strategy and boldness to not hide You away but to share who You are with the world.

Day 67- Not Going Down with the Ship

For You, Lord, are good, and ready to forgive, And abundant in lovingkindness to all who call upon You (Psalm 86:5).

Therefore repent and return, so that your sins may be wiped away, in order that times of refreshing may come from the presence of the Lord (Acts 3:19).

One night I had a dream where I was interviewing the makers and crew of the *Titanic*. They were expressing to me their regrets for some of the choices and mistakes they had made. But I was speaking with one of them about forgiveness and making the choice to let go of the mistakes of the past and move forward. Sadly, this person shook their head no, and I knew they were resolved to continue to go down with the ship.

What God showed me from that dream is that we cannot allow ourselves to be trapped in a place of bondage or where we are unable to progress forward simply because we have invested a lot in our past choices or mistakes.

The more we invest of our heart and resources, the harder it often is to let go of that thing. We can become like that person from my dream where we feel the choices or mistakes we made were so costly to ourselves and to others that we feel we have to continue on with them, even when the ship may be going down. We become both comfortable with our past choices and with the resulting outcome.

But God, in His grace, offers a different outcome. We don't have to go down with the ship no matter how much we have invested in it, sang its praises, brought our friends and family on board with us, told everyone it is indestructible or set our minds on it being the magical vehicle that would bring everyone into a better future.

Nothing man-made and man-promoted is indestructible. But there is forgiveness and grace and opportunity after opportunity to let go of the past, accept forgiveness and move forward to what brings life rather than death!

God has thrown out a life preserver with our name on it, we just need to take hold of it!

Prayer Focus

Jesus, I thank You for Your forgiveness. I ask You to help me in any places that I need to forgive others or myself and let go of things from the past.

Day 68- Redemptive Obedience

Jesus answered and said to him, "If anyone loves Me, he will keep My word; and My Father will love him, and We will come to him and make Our abode with him" (John 14:23).

Obedience will take us places our passion and dreams never will.

It will take us into the places of our "no" and "I'll never" and "there is nothing good there" and give us new lenses.

God is the Great Redeemer, and the reality is He doesn't need to redeem the places we already love and say yes to!

Many in today's society are not big fans of the word obedience. It sometimes triggers childhood hurts and memories of abuse of power. But it is in the places of obedience that you will meet God as Redeemer.

You will find yourself in Nazareth where it was said nothing good could come from it, in Nineveh where you didn't believe it was worth saving, or before the lepers of the day whom you have been instructed to not touch or interact with.

There will be resistance. There will be stretching, and it will come primarily from your own depths!

But in those places, God will show resurrection power that only comes through dying to your no's and to the places you deny knowing Him. He will breathe life over the unthinkable. But it won't be the places your dreams led you because your dreams won't lead down the uncomfortable road to the cross. Only love and obedience and risking it all falling apart will lead you there.

We give obedience a bad report because it is pretty much guaranteed to involve things we don't want to do, and as humans we do like our comfort.

It is time we see obedience for what it is, an act of love and an invitation to redeem what we have put up veils against. Because where we have veils and walls, we have limits on where and how we can move and how God can use us.

In the upside-down kingdom of God, obedience to the One you can trust is the road to tearing down the veils and bringing freedom!

Prayer Focus

God, help me to step past any resistance in my life and walk in obedience.

Day 69- The Return Home

"So he got up and came to his father. But while he was still a long way off, his father saw him and felt compassion for him, and ran and embraced him and kissed him" (Luke 15:20).

Growing up we had a dog named Ashley, and when we would leave town, we always tried to book her into this one "executive" pet center. At this center, the dogs each had a big indoor space that attached to an outdoor run where they could go in and out as they pleased. Ashley loved it because she could roll around in the dirt and run around with other dogs, which she didn't get to do too much at home. The Executive Pet Center cost twice as much as normal boarding places, but we were willing to pay the extra for her to be happy and well taken care of in our absence.

On pick up day, I always watched for the moment when I called her name and she heard my voice. Her ears would perk up and she would turn and get that first sight of us.

She would start running toward us with her tail wagging as fast as it could. She wouldn't be able to contain her excitement and the reunion would be one of sloppy dog kisses and whimpers and her following behind us everywhere we went for the rest of the day.

No matter how nice that executive center was, to Ashley it didn't begin to compare to the company of the ones to whom she belonged. Everything else paled and was quickly forgotten in comparison.

To me, this is like life with God. No matter how good or exciting other things can be, nothing compares to His presence.

And the Father is just like I was, waiting for that moment when His kids get that first sight of Him after being away, or hear His voice for the first time in a long time. Or when we see or hear Him in a way we never have before and we are super excited. It is as special of a moment for Him as it is for us. He never gets tired of seeing us perk up in excitement and He always welcomes our sloppy affection! This is family, this is love.

Prayer Focus

Father, I thank You for how You love me, care for me, and delight in me. May I never lose sight of that.

Day 70- The Master Gardener

"Consider the lilies, how they grow: they neither toil nor spin; but I tell you, not even Solomon in all his glory clothed himself like one of these" (Luke 12:27).

Where you are planted matters, for it will often affect what you produce, as different soils yield different crops.

I love the hydrangeas bush because, with the exception of the pure white ones (which will always remain white), the color of their flower is determined by the pH and mineral content of the soil they are planted in.

Hydrangeas can be pink, blue, purple or white. Their appearance will be transformed simply by transplanting them to different soil or adding different minerals.

We are much like those hydrangeas. What is brought out in us is often dependent on where we are located or what we are exposed to.

I have learned that often when God transplants people to a new location, or brings in something new to their environment, it is for the purpose of bringing something new out of them. They may be unaware that potential is even in them, but suddenly when something new is added, or they are moved into a new environment, a new color makes its way to their surface.

When God changes things up, or moves you, don't be afraid. He is the Master Gardener and knows exactly what you need to bloom! He delights in clothing you in His glory.

Prayer Focus

God, thank You that I can trust that You know what is best for me, and You know exactly what I need to become all You have created me to be. Thank You for shaping and re-shaping my life.

Day 71- No Lack in the Kingdom

It shall come about, if you listen obediently to my commandments which I am commanding you today, to love the LORD your God and to serve Him with all your heart and all your soul, that He will give the rain for your land in its season, the early and late rain, that you may gather in your grain and your new wine and your oil (Deuteronomy 11:13-14).

During a drought a plant must push its roots deeper into the soil to find life-sustaining water. The roots are forced to venture out farther into places they would not normally go if water was readily available.

In times of drought and famine, people often find themselves having to get more creative with their resources. Forming new partnerships, sharing and trading, and learning to work together for the survival of all.

But before any of this can be done, we have to push past the resistance and frustration at not finding the water or food where we thought we would find it. Of things not being readily available, or of things not being in our own storehouse of resources.

It is in these times when we feel lack, that we must make a conscious effort to push our roots out deeper. To move outside of ourself and our familiar territory. We must begin to see with new eyes and ask ourselves what do I have that could meet another person's needs, and what do they have that I need and open a new dialogue.

We tend to undervalue what we ourselves have to offer, but God has given each and every one of us gifts and resources.

God supplies what we need for each season, but some of those resources may be sitting in the storehouses of the people around us.

One may have the knowledge and know how, one may have the monetary resources, another may have the trained work force, and another may have the facilities, but all need to learn to work together for all to progress forward.

God's kingdom is not a kingdom of lack, but sometimes it requires collaboration and creativity for us to tap into or sustain all that is available.

Prayer Focus

God, in times when it looks like I don't have all I need, help me to expand my vision to see where You want me to reach out into new territory and partnership. Give me Your vision.

Day 72- The Birthing

Thus says the LORD who made you And formed you from the womb, who will help you, 'Do not fear, O Jacob My servant; And you Jeshurun whom I have chosen" (Isaiah 44:2).

Behold, children are a gift of the LORD, The fruit of the womb is a reward (Psalm 127:3).

There is a great purge that comes when you transition to the new. It pulls with it everything that was previously sustaining life: the placenta, the umbilical cord, all the fluid and nutrients that were providing warmth and a cushion. It all comes out in one messy swoop as the final pushes of labor occur.

As a baby comes out of the birth canal, it has no idea what is at the end of the canal, but there is no stopping the forward momentum at that point.

At the end of every birth canal, where there was darkness and unknown, suddenly there is light and the new.

New sights, new smells, new experiences. At first, it is all a bit shocking and overwhelming. But then you find yourself being fed and comforted in a new way.

We cannot fear the new and the unknown that God is birthing us into.

When you are in those final stages of life-bringing transition, it is good to keep your focus off of all that you are losing and having to let go. The discomfort, uncertainty, and disorientation that comes with the new territory is only temporary.

Prayer Focus

God, thank You for the transitions of life. Help me to let go of depending on what previously sustained me and turn my focus to Your source for today.

Day 73- Big Promises

God is not a man, that He should lie, Nor a son of man, that He should repent; Has He said, and will He not do it? Or has He spoken, and will He not make it good? (Numbers 23:9).

"Who has heard such a thing? Who has seen such things? Can a land be born in one day? Can a nation be brought forth all at once? As soon as Zion travailed, she also brought forth her sons. "Shall I bring to the point of birth and not give delivery?" says the LORD. "Or shall I who gives delivery shut the womb?" says your God (Isaiah 66:8-9).

Abraham and Sarah's destiny was so big that it would take a wait of a lifetime for that baby to be birthed.

The lineage of Christ and God's entire governmental structure through the twelve tribes of Israel depended on Abraham becoming the father of nations. But first, Abraham and Sarah had to become to parents of one, a baby birthed through their own union.

Sometimes the promises people carry are very big, having the potential to impact generations. These types of promises have a much longer incubation period.

An elephant's gestation is nearly two years long because a baby of that size is not knit together in a short period of time.

When there are long delays, sometimes we need to remind ourselves of the size of the promise.

Your wait time may not be because you have done something wrong to mess things up, because your heart isn't right, or because God has forgotten, is punishing you, or has changed His mind. Your wait might be because of the SIZE of your baby!

Be encouraged for God is faithful. The promise will soon be delivered!

Prayer Focus

God, help me continue to believe that You will do what You said You will do. Give me strength and courage in the time of waiting.

Day 74- Keep Dreaming

My eyes stay open through the watches of the night, that I may meditate on your promises (Psalm 119:148 NIV).

Shortly after the Covid-19 pandemic hit the US, I was watching an interview on TV where a wedding planner was talking about all the cancelled weddings and how her business has flatlined.

She said to the host, "I know when this is all over, there is going to be this big wedding boom. How can I prepare and be ready?"

The host mentioned a few things she could do, but one piece of advice caught my attention. The host said, "What's really important during this time is to keep the brides dreaming. Keep that upcoming wedding before them so that when the time comes, you will be the first person they run to."

This stirred my spirit because I have heard similar words from God so many times when things seemed out of reach.

Keep dreaming. Dream bigger. Don't forget.

It can seem a bit strange to dream about your promises when everything is turned upside down and so much has had to be laid aside. But your dreams and promises are the one thing you cannot afford to lay aside in those times!

When things are looking bleak, it is the time to put your dreams in front of you. To think of how you want things to look. To chart a course. To write out a plan.

The first step in leaping from dream to fulfillment is seeing it!

Prayer Focus

God, help me to keep your promises before me and to keep dreaming. Bring renewed hope to any places where I have begun to doubt or have surrendered your promises.

Day 75- The Sound of Transformation

Then he said to me, "Write, 'Blessed are those who are invited to the marriage supper of the Lamb.'" And he said to me, "These are true words of God." Then I fell at his feet to worship him. But he said to me, "Do not do that; I am a fellow servant of yours and your brethren who hold the testimony of Jesus; worship God. For the testimony of Jesus is the spirit of prophecy (Revelation 19:9-10).

When we speak a testimony of God's goodness in the midst of the pain, it becomes our personal sacrifice of praise, and that praise carries power to transform and reproduce a testimony of its kind.

Heaven hears the sound and recognizes the value and authority of it. The enemy also hears it and to him, it sounds like defeat.

The greater the cost and sacrifice, the greater the transformative power carried on the testimony.

Jesus' blood carried on it the world's pain and betrayal making it the most powerful substance alive.

The testimony of Jesus—his pain, his sacrifice, his overcoming and the proclamation of the goodness of God in the midst of it— IS the spirit of prophecy.

We can release a sound of testimony that shakes a nation, that carries healing, that carries freedom, that carries transformation. But first we have to recognize the value of what is produced, and then proclaimed in those hard and sacrificial times.

After his denial of Jesus recorded in the gospels, the Apostle Peter took what had to be great disappointment, pain of his own failure and betrayal and turned and proclaimed God's goodness to the tune of great power, boldness and authority. As a result, thousands came to the knowledge of Christ.

Life will always hold disappointments, pain, betrayal, and what we deem as failures. But, when we encounter these things, we need to recognize them for what they are, an opportunity to release a new sound, to upgrade your testimony, to proclaim the goodness of God and see that there is still redemptive power in the shed blood of Christ!

Prayer Focus

God, help me to proclaim Your goodness and share my testimonies of the power of Christ's redemption in my life, so that others may hear and their lives be transformed.

Day 76- The Harvest Fields

Then He said to His disciples, "The harvest is plentiful, but the workers are few. Therefore beseech the Lord of the harvest to send out workers into His harvest" (Mathew 9:37-38).

Who dares despise the day of small things, since the seven eyes of the LORD that range throughout the earth will rejoice when they see the chosen capstone in the hand of Zerubbabel? (Zechariah 4:10 NIV).

The harvest is a multifaceted picture.

You have harvests from fields that stretch out for miles, and then you have little backyard or even window gardens. All produce a harvest.

Sometimes the fruit from that little backyard harvest is even sweeter than that from larger harvest fields, and may have taken more work to grow. God looks upon it all and calls it good. And He has a purpose for it all.

Years ago, God took me to the hot climate growing fields in Australia's Hunter Valley. In the vineyards there, there are less grapes and they have to be spaced out on the vines to endure the prolonged heat and drought conditions.

The following year, He took me to the cold climate growing fields in Canada where they produce ice wine. There, the grapes are saturated, crushed while frozen to produce highly concentrated, low yield, and therefore, high-cost wines.

In both of these pictures of harvest, neither could produce large yields of wine that could be mass produced and sold in big box stores. Because of the growing conditions, the makers of these wines had to sacrifice big yield for their quality of wine. But that increased the value of the wine.

Sometimes in our journey with Christ we can get frustrated with the lack of big "results." But God reminds us that there are different harvest fields and different qualities of wine.

Smaller harvest fields are unattractive to most because of the lower yield, the unattractive ratio of work versus fruit. But they are important to the harvest because of the investment and quality of what they produce.

In our day, most measure success by volume, not by heart, effort or cost. But God sees the entire picture. Jesus said that widow's contribution of a mite (equivalent of a single cent) was greater than all the other contributors to the treasury because she put in all she had.

If you are one called to spend your life cultivating a garden that nourishes and brings life to a single rare treasure to be harvested, God values and rejoices over your harvest like

He does the one who stands on a stage or over a media platform and reaches tens of thousands. Don't despise the size of your harvest field, allow God to place you in the field that He sees fit for you at this time in your life.

Prayer Focus

God, help me to not judge by number, or by man's way of measuring. Let me value my harvest field, big or small.

Day 77- Staying in Motion

Now the LORD said to Abram, "Go forth from your country, And from your relatives And from your father's house, To the land which I will show you" (Genesis 12:1).

In my walk with God, one of the things He often repeats is to keep moving even if I am uncertain exactly where I'm headed.

In times of uncertainty, we tend to want to pause and stop until we can get clear direction. In fact, that is advice I hear in all the time. But we fail to take into account the Law of Inertia. This law says an object that is not in movement will resist the change toward movement. It will have more forces to overcome to get moving again. But an object that is already moving will have less resistance and redirecting its motion is easier than getting it to move again once it has stopped.

If we allow ourselves to be paralyzed by fear, error or the unknown, or we sit around waiting for full clarity on how to proceed, we are less likely to get back in the game even when we gain clarity on which direction we should go. The obstacles toward getting moving will seem insurmountable.

God is a master at redirecting and getting us to where we need to be. He is constantly recalibrating and redirecting our steps, but He needs movement to work with!

Go to the land which I will show you, step into the waters of the Jordan, feed the 5000, get out of the boat and come to me on the water. None of these commands came with a clear picture of how things were going to work or a guarantee from God on what He was going to do. But each of them set the people in motion. From there, God would co-labor with them and work His miracles!

Prayer Focus

God, help me to go when You say go, even when there is uncertainty. Help me to trust that You will guide me and to keep moving until You say stop.

Day 78- Little Foxes

Catch the foxes for us, The little foxes that are ruining the vineyards, While our vineyards are in blossom (Song of Solomon 2:15).

"The thief comes only to steal and kill and destroy; I came that they may have life, and have it abundantly" (John 10:10).

Often, we can find ourselves like Esau in the book of Genesis, trading our birthright and inheritance for that which brings quick gain or relief to the hunger of the day.

In our fear, our fatigue, our loneliness and impatience of the hour, we must be careful not to give ground and let the enemy steal what is rightfully ours.

It is often through the little areas of compromise that he steals the most, because we convince ourselves that in the big scheme of things, a little compromise won't matter. And the enemy is good at convincing us of how dire the temporary situation is.

Esau told Jacob, *"Behold, I am about to die; so of what use then is the birthright to me?" (Genesis 25:32)*. I'm pretty sure that Esau was not about to die, but he had tunnel vision and could only focus on what he wanted in the moment.

We can't let popular opinion of what we should do, pressure from man, or the lure of temporary relief cause us to compromise much greater things.

There is precious fruit beginning to grow on the vines. But those little foxes will gnaw through the vines and steal away the crop before it is mature for harvest!

Prayer Focus

God, show me if there are any areas of compromise that might cause me to forfeit what You have for me. Help me to walk in full integrity.

Day 79- Look Up

When they had crossed over, Elijah said to Elisha, "Ask what I shall do for you before I am taken from you." And Elisha said, "Please, let a double portion of your spirit be upon me." He said, "You have asked a hard thing. Nevertheless, if you see me when I am taken from you, it shall be so for you; but if not, it shall not be so" (2 Kings 2:9-10).

A few years ago, as I watched the launch of the Falcon 9 rocket, 2 Kings 2:9-10 immediately came to mind. It's where the prophet Elisha asks Elijah for a double portion of his spirit upon him. In other words, he asked him for the inheritance of the firstborn son.

Elijah told him that he had asked a difficult thing because, of course, Elisha was not his firstborn son and that would be usurping the natural order of things. But he told him that if he saw him when he was taken from him, that inheritance could be his.

This picture was also seen with Jesus and his disciples in Chapter 1 of the book of Acts when the disciples asked Jesus if it was time for the kingdom to be restored to Israel. Jesus told them that it was not for them to know the time, but that they would receive power when the Holy Spirit came upon them to be His witnesses in the earth. The disciples then stood and watched intently as He was lifted into the sky just as Elijah had previously been taken into the sky.

The disciples then went to the upper room where there they received a double portion inheritance as the Spirit fell upon them.

If you have vision to seize it, the inheritance of the firstborn son (Jesus) can be yours. You can usurp even natural order. If you can see Him in the hour when He seems to have departed from you, His Spirit will come to you in a new way that will empower you for the work of seeing the kingdom restored!

For those who stick close by His side, and look up and watch intently, the promised impartation of new power and authority is always at hand!

Prayer Focus

Jesus, help us to look up and focus on You to receive our inheritances.

Day 80- Believing with a Whole Heart

And He took him outside and said, "Now look toward the heavens, and count the stars, if you are able to count them." And He said to him, "So shall your descendants be." Then he believed in the LORD; and He reckoned it to him as righteousness (Genesis 15:5-6).

In our human nature, there is a part of us that wants to self-protect and hold back a piece of our heart in case our faith journey doesn't work out the way we are hoping. We want to wait to tell others about it until we know it's a sure thing or after until after the victory. We don't want to be embarrassed, look like a fool, or be left with egg on our face.

But holding back is kind of like living life with a divorce mentality. That you will only give God your all if you can be assured that it will be everything you want and more. But really, if it's guaranteed, faith isn't required!

In Genesis, when God told Abram that his descendants would be like the stars, the Bible says that Abram believed God. That word believed here means he carried it, fostered it, and made it firm.

And because of how Abram (later called Abraham) carried and moved upon God's word, God counted it as righteousness. Yet Abraham was at the beginning of this generational story.

He would be one to pass the promise to his son without getting to see all those descendants himself. He and Sarah only had one son together.

But Abraham can teach us a lesson because the heavens still declare his name. The seeds he planted are still on the earth. Without his part, none of our parts would have come into existence.

In our world, we tend to only look at life from within our generation, and tend to only give the medal of victory to the ones who got to cross the proverbial finish line and hold the spoils of the victory. But God sits outside of time and sees the first the same as the last. To Him, the heart and effort put into what you contributed is so much more valuable than the medal and outcome itself.

Avoid the temptation to hold back a part of your heart. To not risk big so that you won't be hurt big. To be driven only if you can hold the spoils.

Prayer Focus

God, help me to resolve in my heart today that no matter the potential outcome, I will carry Your word and promises with every fiber of my being.

Day 81- Walking in the Garden

They heard the sound of the LORD God walking in the garden in the cool of the day, and the man and his wife hid themselves from the presence of the LORD God among the trees of the garden. Then the LORD God called to the man, and said to him, "Where are you?" (Genesis 3:8-9).

Growing up, my father had a coffee routine.

Each morning he would grind the beans and carefully brew the coffee. While it was brewing, he would wash up any stray dishes from the night before.

As I grew older, he would make the coffee for two, and I would join him. Then he would run the dish water, but often I would be the one to come in and wash the dishes. It was never discussed. It just happened that way, in the coming together of the moment.

It would be a couple hours before anyone else in the house stirred, so during that time, my dad and I would sit out in the garden or on the porch and drink our coffee and talk about everything under the sun. Even after I bought my own home, often I would drive over in the morning for coffee time together. My dad has since gone to heaven, but I still greatly miss our coffee time.

My heavenly Father and I also have our own morning routine. He wakes me up early, normally between 2:00 and 4:00 and we talk about many things. It's not a time of worship or prayer. It is a time where He shares His heart, and often I share mine or ask questions. If there is a day when this morning chat time doesn't happen, I feel the loss of it, and He does too and will call out to me when I go missing, like He did to Adam in the garden of Eden.

Sometimes the biggest, most meaningful encounters with God are not at a church service or a conference, but in those times He treasures most, when you will walk in the cool of the garden with just Him. No crowds, no entertainment, no distractions, no agenda. It is in those places that He will share the secrets of the universe!

Prayer Focus

Father, thank You for those intimate spaces You invite me into. Thank You that I can enjoy Your presence one on one.

Day 82- The Legacy of the Father

Tell of His glory among the nations, His wonderful deeds among all the peoples (1Chronicles 16:24).

For the LORD takes pleasure in His people; He will beautify the afflicted ones with salvation (Psalm 149:4).

"Do not be afraid, little flock, for your Father has chosen gladly to give you the kingdom" (Luke 12:32).

Years ago, when I was in Germany, I contacted the caretaker of Dietrich Bonhoeffer's home, a family member of his, and arranged a visit.

Downstairs in what was once a ballroom, they had set up family pictures and historical accounts. The walls held Dietrich's story.

Over the years, God has often mentioned Dietrich to me, but one day He was talking to me about legacy, and brought to mind not Dietrich, but the caretaker of his home.

This caretaker had probably opened that home and given hundreds of tours over the years to theologians, revivalists and passers-by. A story that never really changes, yet as he spoke, he wept and talked about how much of an honor it was to spend his life sharing the story and legacy of Dietrich.

Dietrich's legacy had become his own, and each telling helped keep that legacy alive to be passed on. Decades had not wiped it away from the caretaker's heart, the walls of that home, or the history books around the world.

In the same fashion that the Father loves to hear stories of His son Jesus, He loves to hear stories of His other sons and daughters. Our legacy is their legacy, and it is continued on through generations by those who bear their image.

When we think about the legacy of Christ, we need to realize that it would be impossible to only pass on His legacy. His story intertwines with the Father's and with each of His disciples and countless people He has touched through the generations. So, to share His legacy is also to share theirs and our own.

The miraculous testimonies of how God has moved in our life don't just belong to us. They are the continuing legacy of the Creator of the universe, a God who heals, saves and delivers, but even more, a God who calls us His own and is proud that we carry on His legacy.

God brought up the caretaker of Dietrich's home that day as an example of how He views our legacy. He is honored to share His legacy with us, and in turn takes our legacy on as His own. The testimonies never get old to Him. He will spend eternity weeping over them in love.

Prayer Focus

Father, thank You for Your legacy and for inviting us into it. Let me come into the full realization of how much of an honor that is.

Day 83- Sharp and Ready

Iron sharpens iron, So one man sharpens another (Proverbs 27:17).

It is iron that sharpens iron. But in order for this to happen, friction must be allowed in the relationship.

Our mindset can sometimes be one of intolerance to anything that is not full adoration and praise. No questions, no suggestions, no strong wills or push back allowed. No iron to rub up against us.

Rather than realizing the positives of the strength of the iron and nurturing and utilizing its strength, as soon as we come up against it, we want to set it aside, shut it down or push it away in favor of what easily yields and is softer and always feels good.

But one that allows no friction, tension or pruning is one who will never be as sharp or as fruitful as they were intended to be.

Over time, iron that never gets sharpened becomes dull and unable to cut through the very things it was designed to. This dulling becomes the downfall of so many great people and organizations in our day.

It is good to remember that iron is necessary when forming our core circles. Some tension is necessary to mold and sustain you!

Prayer Focus

God, help me to have healthy relationships that leave room for necessary friction, so that I may be strong and shaped into who I am intended to be. Show me any places where I have been resistant to necessary tension and help me to lay that resistance down.

Day 84- Freedom to Not be Free

Now the Lord is the Spirit, and where the Spirit of the Lord is, there is liberty (2 Corinthians 3:17).

Paul, a bond-servant of Christ Jesus, called as an apostle, set apart for the gospel of God, which He promised beforehand through His prophets in the holy Scriptures (Romans 1:1-2).

In the book of Acts, chapter 16, there is an amazing account of the Apostle Paul and Silas, who after being beaten and wrongfully imprisoned began to pray and sing hymns of praise. While they were doing this, there was a great earthquake that shook the prison opening all the prison doors and freeing all the prisoners' chains. Surely, this was an act of God offering them their freedom.

But what is so amazing about this account is they made the choice to not take the offer. They cared more about the wellbeing of the man who jailed them than they did about their own freedom. They knew that the man would come to harm if they escaped, so they stayed, risking him coming and re-locking the jail cell.

This act of selflessness was so stunning to the jailer that it made him instantly believe in God. And not just the jailer, but his entire household!

Funny thing about freedom, sometimes the laying down of freedom and rights of one allows other captives to be set free. Wasn't this the very picture Jesus demonstrated?

John 15:13 says, *"Greater love has no one than this, that one lay down his life for his friends."* But what about your so-called enemies?

The Apostle Paul called himself a bondservant (slave) of Christ. Giving the picture that he had laid down his freedoms to follow Jesus.

The love of the Father that Jesus, Paul and Silas displayed was so big that it had room even for the ones who had beaten, mocked and imprisoned them. What a powerful Love!

Prayer Focus

Jesus, I thank You for the freedom You have given us, even the freedom to surrender it for greater gain.

Day 85- Dare to be Specialized

I will give thanks to You, for I am fearfully and wonderfully made; Wonderful are Your works, And my soul knows it very well (Proverbs 139:14).

Remember that every voice is unique. Not only is it unique, but intended to resonate with a particular audience. Your voice will not be for everyone.

Sound and light come in different frequencies. Some that can only be heard or seen by certain species.

Maybe your voice was created as a sound meant to resonate across broad audiences, but maybe your voice is like that of a dog whistle, limited to a few species, or like the sound of a humpback whale, only understood by one kind. If that is you, dare to be specialized!

Don't spend your life trying to be heard by an audience that is not yours. Often in man's quest to try and broaden their reach, they lose their original audience, the very audience they were created for. Then we end up with an oversaturation of the same sound reaching the same audiences, and sadly, whole groups that never hear the sounds that resonate with their being and let them know they are not alone.

Your success is not determined by the size of the audience you reach. Your success is determined by you meeting the objective for which you were created, whether that is being a voice to one, or being a voice to millions.

Prayer Focus

God, I thank You for how You have designed me. Help me to fully realize my voice and place me where it will be heard, resonate and bring transformation.

Day 86- Kingdom Multiplication

Now a certain woman of the wives of the sons of the prophets cried out to Elisha, "Your servant my husband is dead, and you know that your servant feared the LORD; and the creditor has come to take my two children to be his slaves." Elisha said to her, "What shall I do for you? Tell me, what do you have in the house?" And she said, "Your maidservant has nothing in the house except a jar of oil." Then he said, "Go, borrow vessels at large for yourself from all your neighbors, even empty vessels; do not get a few. And you shall go in and shut the door behind you and your sons, and pour out into all these vessels, and you shall set aside what is full." So she went from him and shut the door behind her and her sons; they were bringing the vessels to her and she poured. And it came about when the vessels were full, that she said to her son, "Bring me another vessel." And he said to her, "There is not one vessel more." And the oil stopped. Then she came and told the man of God. And he said, "Go, sell the oil and pay your debt, and you and your sons can live on the rest" (2 Kings 4:1-7).

"Give, and it will be given to you. They will pour into your lap a good measure— pressed down, shaken together, and running over. For by your standard of measure it will be measured to you in return" (Luke 6:38).

"Tell me, what do you have in the house?"

This is the question the prophet Elisha asked the widow. What did she already have on hand, for that would be her seed for multiplication.

He instructed her first to gather empty vessels, and then to pour into them.

God is a god of multiplication, and this is still the principle at hand. Use what you have available, no matter how little you think it is. Find those who are empty and pour into them, and God will be faithful to fill each one that you have brought. Then, you are to live off the excess.

When things are looking a bit thin and hopeless, we often cry out like that widow for rescue, and God answers much like Elisha did.

Elisha was essentially telling the widow, you don't need me to rescue you. You have the power and ability to bring your own increase. He didn't pay her debts for her. Instead, he taught her how to live the rest of her days in abundance.

If we only look to continually receive from others, we will just be temporarily filled to empty out again and again. But rather you are to pour out, and for each vessel you are willing to pour into, more will be given to you!

Prayer Focus

God, help me to learn to multiply what You have given me and to walk in abundance.

Day 87- Springboards and Instruments

For momentary, light affliction is producing for us an eternal weight of glory far beyond all comparison (2 Corinthians 4:17).

Tension can be a good thing in life. Our areas of tension can function as our springboards to propel us forward.

You don't have a springboard without tension.
You don't have a bow to shoot an arrow without tension.
You don't have a slingshot without tension.
You don't have a rocket launch without a great push against the gravitation forces.

Sometimes, we are asking God why we haven't been launched into what He has promised, and the answer is because we haven't been willing to endure the tension or the heat of the launch to get our breakthrough.

To break through, you have to not only come up against a set boundary, but you have to be willing to push up against it until it breaks.

Sometimes, we can find ourselves crying out to God for less tension in our lives, but He knows that what we really need is more, not less, in order to breakthrough. But that tension must be in the right places!

Like a stringed instrument, tension in the right places will produce a beautiful sound. But too much tension will leave you out of tune, or even break the wire.

Let the Holy Spirit be your tuner, telling you where more or less tension is needed.

Prayer Focus

God, help me to walk in balance and be in tune with You. Help me to allow tension where it is needed and to release it where it is not.

Day 88- He is Still God

For the vision is yet for the appointed time; It hastens toward the goal and it will not fail. Though it tarries, wait for it; For it will certainly come, it will not delay (Habakkuk 2:4).

Few babies are born into the picture-perfect birth we imagined they would be. Despite the knowledge of an impending birth, talking about it for months, and all the planning, birthing classes and books read, thousands of babies are still birthed in cars, on the side of the road, in kitchens and bathrooms and inconvenient public places with no birthing coach or support in sight.

When a promise is close to its time of fulfillment, God will increase talk about the impending birth. But in those times, we don't always see the signs that we are in a birthing room. So, we may think this thing isn't getting ready to happen or that life has moved on. We may start to work on plan B.

We forget that babies come at inconvenient, often unexpected times. When birth comes on the scene, it disrupts the current priority and what you previously thought was significant.

We cannot let the chaos or the routine of everyday life fool us into thinking God is not going to deliver!

Perhaps you are beyond your due date. Perhaps you have had a few false labors and rushed to the birthing center just to leave in disappointment each time. YOU may have set things aside and returned to other things, but on your way to the grocery store, while driving to work, or in the wee hours of the night, promises arrive and God reminds us that HE IS STILL GOD!

Prayer Focus

God, help me to stay expectant and ready for the birthing of Your promises.

Day 89- The Bugler

Out of the heavens He let you hear His voice to discipline you; and on earth He let you see His great fire, and you heard His words from the midst of the fire (Deuteronomy 4:36).

For He is our God, And we are the people of His pasture and the sheep of His hand. Today, if you would hear His voice, Do not harden your hearts, as at Meribah, As in the day of Massah in the wilderness (Psalm 95:7-8).

Years ago, I used to live at a Naval Station, and each morning my day would start with the sound of the bugler playing. When this happened, for some reason I would find myself looking at the clock to see if he was on-time.

The bugler was never late.

The community where I lived was a mix of civilians and military. And I'm sure the majority of the civilians who lived there had long tuned out the daily calls. But not those whom they were meant for, those who were trained to listen for them and to know what each one meant. Those who set their lives by them.

God began to stir my heart about this because life with Him is much like those calls. It is God who announces the time. Many tune out the announcements, but some actually tune their ears to listen for them and hear what they are announcing so that they can move in step with Him and be at the right place at the right time.

Being in tune with God and hearing His daily direction is essential to our lives and wellbeing.

Sometimes we can allow other noises and wrong voices to arrange our lives and crowd out what we should be listening for and we will quickly fall out of step. But the good news is we can always re-condition our ear to listen for the Bugler. Rain or shine, God will faithfully announce to His people direction for the day.

Prayer Focus

God, help me to hear Your voice and never tune it out. Help me to not be distracted by other noises and voices around me.

Day 90- Unseen Impact

I will sing of lovingkindness and justice, To You, O LORD, I will sing praises (Psalm 101:1).

"Then I will sprinkle clean water on you, and you will be clean; I will cleanse you from all your filthiness and from all your idols" (Ezekiel 36:25).

Years ago, I was driving home, fully engaged in singing along with the worship song that was playing in my car. Suddenly, out of nowhere God decided to allow me to see in the spirit.

My vision shifted and there on that highway, I could suddenly see the impact of my song. It looked like soap suds that went out and covered everything it encountered. Not just inside my car, but covering all the cars around me. The suds dripped down the surrounding vehicles. It was as if they were being washed because the suds changed the colors of the people and objects as they dripped down.

The experience probably lasted less than a minute, but it forever changed my view on worship and the power of the words we speak.

Prior to that day, I had never considered that the sounds I released, sounds that those in the other cars around me likely could not even hear, were impacting those around me. To me, I was just worshipping in my car like I always do.

But sound impacts matter even when it is not heard.

Often we can't see our full impact on the world. While we think we are just going about life, making little difference, we impact and change more than we know.

The people in those cars around me that day would have had no explanation for the changes I saw in the spirit. Maybe as the suds of my song washed over them their mood suddenly felt lighter, or maybe they felt peace or God touch them in some other way. I don't know. But God wanted me to be aware that there was unseen impact.

In the natural, we don't get to see what we push out into the atmosphere, but know that you do push something out, good or bad. So let it be that which gives life!

Prayer Focus

God, give me greater revelation of the impact of my voice and my life. Let me not doubt its transformative power.

Made in the USA
Las Vegas, NV
14 August 2023

76087307R00116